NOIR
BY
NECESSITY

How My Father's Unsolved Murder Took Me to Dark Places

MIKE GATTO

Black Rose Writing | Texas

The author grants the final approval for this literary material.

First printing

In many instances where possible without sacrificing accuracy, the author has omitted names to preserve certain people's anonymity.

ISBN: 978-1-68513-381-8
LIBRARY OF CONGRESS CONTROL NUMBER: 2023948141
PUBLISHED BY BLACK ROSE WRITING
www.blackrosewriting.com

Printed in the United States of America
Suggested Retail Price (SRP) $20.95

Noir by Necessity is printed in Minion Pro

*As a planet-friendly publisher, Black Rose Writing does its best to eliminate unnecessary waste to reduce paper usage and energy costs, while never compromising the reading experience. As a result, the final word count vs. page count may not meet common expectations.

PRAISE FOR

NOIR
BY
NECESSITY

"The murder of a family member causes incredible pain, no matter whether the killer was someone like Charles Manson or just a random assailant. Kudos to Assemblyman Gatto for ripping off the band-aid, to give people a sense of what it's like. This is an important book for anyone who cares about True Crime sagas."

–Debra Tate, sister of Manson Family victim, actress Sharon Tate

"The murder of Joseph Gatto captivated Los Angeles. Many veteran journalists still wonder how and why it happened. The details of this horrible crime and those affected by it continue to fascinate."

–Robert Kovacik, Anchor and Reporter, NBC Los Angeles

"A deeply honest and compelling account of Gatto's journey - personal and political - in the aftermath of his father's shocking murder. While the details, including his high profile job, are unique, it's also a universal narrative reflecting the yearning and pain of survivors of unsolved crimes."

–Marisa Lagos, Politics and Crime Correspondent, KQED

To all the family members of murder victims,
searching for answers.

Special Thanks to
Jason Insalaco & Matthew Sharp

NOIR
BY
NECESSITY

PREFACE

Death is part of life. Everyone loses a loved one at some point. However, when most people lose a loved one, they get a chance to say goodbye. And they know why and how their loved one died.

Cancer, for example, is tremendously hard on families. But if a loved one gets cancer, the family usually gets to comfort the afflicted, resolve burning questions, grudgingly accept how the disease unfolds, and say their goodbyes.

A murder, however, particularly an unsolved one, robs the family of the dignity and solace that those rites of passage can provide. In addition to being a most traumatic way to lose a loved one, you don't get to offer the deceased any comfort. You can't hold their hands or reassure them as they pass from one world to another. You never get to say goodbye.

And in many cases, you don't even know basic facts, like how—or why—they had to die.

My father was murdered in November 2013. I'd provide you the exact date, but we're not even sure if it was on the 12th or the 13th. As of writing, the killer or killers have not been identified. Nobody has been brought to justice.

We have clues of course—some tantalizing. I've spent many days collecting them and many nights agonizing over them. Through it all, one of the most difficult things (in addition to losing my father) has been the lack of answers.

I believe it might help people put themselves in the shoes of families like mine if I lay this book out with this purpose. In a world where much attention is paid to whether criminals are getting the right treatment, victims' families continue to be overlooked. Stories focus on the guilt of the possible perpetrators or the finite details of the moment a murder happened, and ignore the fallout borne by the departed's living loved ones. Therefore, this book is not structured to synthesize information for the reader.

Instead, it's chronological chaos. It's laid out to allow the reader go through the same steps, feel the same emotions, and learn the same tidbits of information and clues, in the same order I did. Your knowledge in this book—the leads, the tips, the false starts—will unfold on these pages, just as it has for me in real life.

Because I present the material chronologically, in a series of vignettes dating from my father's passing, certain relevant memories are weaved in as flashbacks, or lengthy asides. I did that to preserve the structure for the reader, of learning the clues, undergoing the experiences, feeling the emotions, and recalling and reflecting, all in the same order I did.

My sincere hope is that none of my readers ever experience losing a loved one at the hands of a murderer. But with this book, that you gain an understanding of what families of murder victims go through and carry with them every day.

STATUS QUO ANTE

I do not remember any other one-year period of my life when I had been as happy as I was during the twelve months or so leading up to my father's murder. In October 2012, my second daughter was born, a charismatic and beautiful baby girl we named Evangelina, but whose two-and-a-half-year-old sister, Elliana, called her, "schmookie bookie." (The second half of that nickname stuck, and let me tell you, it raises some eyebrows when an very Italian-looking father calls his little girl "Bookie" in public.)

I had been through six bruising campaigns for the California legislature, but had prevailed in each, and was focused wholly on something I loved: the job of governance. I was Chairman of the powerful Appropriations Committee, arguably the fourth most powerful elected job in the state, after the Governor and the leaders of each legislative house.

I was very happy in my marriage to my wife Danielle, and we had settled into political life finally, and overcome some challenging times we had had a few years before.

Even our finances were in good order, despite the pay cut I had taken leaving the private sector for elected life. In the past year we had traveled to Europe, and managed to buy a little duplex to rent out.

My relationship with my parents was also better than ever. They had divorced after 24 years of marriage, but still lived close to one another and to us. They both were enjoying their golden years, loving the freedom of retirement and spending time with their grandkids. I was close to both of them, and both had helped me tremendously in my campaigns, by calling voters, delivering lawn signs, and walking door to door for votes. I was a grateful son, and I believe they were proud of me.

During this period, I specifically remember reflecting (often on one of the innumerable plane rides I took) on just how fortunate I was. I was doing what I loved, making a difference, and living in a house full of love.

In October 2013, I turned 39 years old, and remember thinking that I could enjoy the last year of my thirties on the top of the world.

I was wrong.

November 11, 2013

My week started as it had typically done during my time in office. The California Legislature is full time. I often explain to people that we were required to be in the Capitol roughly whenever kids are in school. Thus, I had settled into a rhythm of spending weekdays in our

Sacramento house and weekends in my district, which covered Burbank, Glendale, and several Los Angeles neighborhoods like Hollywood, Los Feliz, and Silver Lake. My wife Danielle and our two toddler daughters stayed mostly in Sacramento, a practice that could be politically detrimental, but I didn't mind. I wanted them to have stability, so I didn't want to force them to travel back and forth with me, and yet I wanted us to be together as much as possible.

The week of November 10, 2013 was a little different because Monday was a holiday, Veteran's Day, which fell on the 11th in 2013. That day, I stopped by the big Veteran's Day event at the Hall of Liberty at Forest Lawn Hollywood. Next, I addressed the Burbank Veteran's Day ceremony, which was always very well-done. In my speech, I mentioned the veterans who had a profound effect on my life: my two "Uncles" (technically first-cousins, once-removed), decorated combat vets in World War II; another cousin, a Vietnam vet; and my father, who served four years in the Army in the 1950s between Korea and Vietnam.

That afternoon, I got on a flight back to Sacramento, back to my waiting wife and daughters. We had a quiet dinner, and I read them lots of fun stories, as I did every night, as they went to sleep.

November 12

The next day, November 12, was quiet and uneventful. I spent the day making a few fundraising calls, emailing my staff about this or that, and spending time with my girls. There was a nice little park near our Sacramento house, and I walked them to it, and pushed Elliana on the swings. I tried to put politics out of my mind for a bit, to make up for their little-kid poutiness that their daddy had been away from them.

The next weekend, we had plans to take the family to Lake Tahoe with Danielle's best friend, who had also moved from Los Angeles to Sacramento, who had girls the same ages as ours, and lived a few minutes from us. It was going to be a rare break for us, and we hoped the kids would get to see some snow. Danielle and I discussed all the things we were going to do. We were excited, and my oldest daughter could hardly wait to go see Christmas trees growing in the mountains.

November 13

My staff had scheduled my formal portrait session at the Capitol portico first thing in the morning. I had been in office for almost three years at this point, and still had a crappy, informal portrait. While most elected officials take their official portraits a few months after Election Day, after the stress of a campaign has settled down, I had been elected in a Special Election mid-year, and took my pictures a couple days after that victory, in the middle of a term and a colossal budget fight, with no time to catch my breath. I had sprinted ever since—with no breaks.

But that November, I was finally settled in. My tough elections were behind me, Danielle wasn't pregnant, and our newborn of the previous year was finally allowing us to sleep occasionally. Thus, I could finally re-take my portraits, at a quiet day at the Capitol.

After my photo session, I met with the Governor's key budget officials regarding funding to combat an invasive psyllid that was hurting California's important citrus industry. I next met with an education-reform activist, and took a meeting with one of my colleagues who wanted to run for Speaker when the current Speaker's term ended. I chatted with my staff a bit, and went home in the afternoon. On the way home, I called my dad to see if he had a recommendation for a new plumber for my place in Los Angeles. He didn't answer. I left him a voice mail.

I remember that evening vividly. I'm sure some of the events aren't in the proper order, but what happened that night is not stuff you tend to forget.

Baby Evie was already sleeping, and Elliana was chatting with Danielle and I, standing near the kitchen countertop. I was about to put her to bed, which she always insisted on, but my cell phone rang. It was my younger sister, Mariann. She was talking rapidly and very loudly. She said something like, "Michael, I went over to dad's house and I found him slumped over in his desk chair. I think he's dead."

I replied with something like, "That can't be! He's in fantastic shape." And this was true. My dad was an absolute beast. He regularly sprinted up stairs at the age of 78. He had more hand strength, and perhaps more strength period, than most twentysomethings. (Danielle was shocked one day when he came over to our house and she opened the door to find him dead-lifting a mid-size refrigerator that he had just carried up the stairs without help.) He had been genetically tested, and had many of the "centenarian" genetic markers. A woman from my father's ancestral hometown in Italy had lived to 112, longevity being common there. My father also had no significant heart or health issues. So, I just couldn't believe that he had died.

My sister then said something like, "there may be a wound, but I can't tell. And he's cold to the touch." To which I said, "well don't just guess—call an ambulance!"

By this time, Danielle was mouthing, "what's wrong?" Wanting to shield Elliana, we distracted her for a second. I then mouthed to Danielle the incredible news: my sister says my dad is dead.

I next made a bunch of calls. I called my District Chief of Staff, Jason Insalaco. At any challenging moment, it's hard to be far away. Thankfully, I had Jason. He was my eyes and ears when I was in the Capitol, and I trusted him with everything. More than just heading my district office, he had also known my family for decades. I explained what I knew: my dad was likely dead, and the EMTs who had since arrived suspected foul play. I asked him to drive to the house to help. He left immediately.

I also called my friend, Los Angeles Councilman Joe Buscaino. He is a former police officer, and was still very close with the LAPD. I told him what was going on, and soon I was in touch with the Chief of Police.

At some point, I got a call from Mariann again or Jason, confirming that my dad was dead, and the cause of death was likely murder.

It was the first and only murder in the quiet, artsy, family-oriented Silver Lake neighborhood that year.

THE FIRST HAZY DETAILS

The next few hours were dizzying. I fielded dozens of calls from police personnel as more tidbits of information came in. I had to call my dad's brothers and first cousins, so they didn't first hear about my dad's death on the news. Those were terribly difficult calls to make. I had to call my staff, and the Speaker of the Assembly, John Perez, to let them know what was going on.

Between the phone calls, the worrying, and the shock, I was up all night.

At some point, a TV van pulled outside our home and erected its large satellite transmitter. They must have gotten our Sacramento address from public records. Danielle called the corresponding news desk and pleaded with them to leave for our safety. Few knew our Sacramento address, and believing that we might also be in danger, we preferred to keep it that way. Nevertheless, rather than accommodating our request, the person who answered the phone attempted to interview Danielle, and the news van stayed put. At some point, the Speaker sent some members of our legislative police force to my house for protection. The night passed in a blur.

The next morning, two very groggy parents threw a few things in a suitcase and drove to LA. We had no idea what awaited us, or how the next several years would affect me so profoundly.

REALITY SETS IN

The Los Angeles of my youth was different from the Los Angeles of 2013. As a child, I remember the entire city living in terror of the Night Stalker, a serial killer who terrorized the city for months. And it wasn't just the high-profile stuff we were afraid of, when I was a kid. In 1992, the year I graduated high school, there were 2,589 homicides in the city. Many neighborhoods, including Silver Lake, were then not considered safe, or even middle-class.

The Los Angeles when my father was a young man was also different. This was the Los Angeles of the Black Dahlia and the Manson Family. One of the houses of the Manson murder victims, the LaBianca house, was walking distance from my father's. My father had taught one of the Manson girls. So his life had been intersected by high-profile murders in the past. (And in a freakish coincidence, my father was killed on Charles Manson's birthday).

I remember conversations with my father about crime. Such conversations occurred regularly, just like conversations about other important issues, like education. While we shared a general sense of fear and unease at the high crime rate in the big city, you never really imagine it will happen to you. You fear it generally. You never expect it individually.

And the Los Angeles of 2013 was more peaceful and idyllic. There were just 251 murders reported that year, a 40-year low.

November 14

As we drove to LA, condolences emails and texts started coming in. The *Los Angeles Times* had come out with a breaking news story, which had hit the news aggregators in the wee hours of the morning. Every couple seconds my phone would ring, or I'd get a text or an email from people offering their condolences, sympathy, or assistance. Governor Jerry Brown called, as did Los Angeles Mayor Eric Garcetti, and dozens of Republicans too. Singer Josh Groban posted condolences on twitter. Senator Feinstein messengered over a card. The news spread fast and far. I even got an email from someone I attended college with, who now lived in faraway Maine. I also got lots of calls and texts from the media. Most went through my office, but a few got to me directly. Danielle fielded quite a few calls too while I drove, and she maintains to this day that Kamala Harris was the most empathetic of them all, calling not as a formality, but with a deep human concern for our suffering.

But the news stories also brought out the weirdos. One lady ("Marje L. LaMar") commented on Facebook, "I am sure it's democrats killing more democrat. (sic.) That's all those people seem to do." Damn, I thought, "I am many things: a father, a son, a husband, a friend, a pretty darn good two-hand-touch football player, and above all, just a fellow human being. And all this person wants is to label me as a 'democrat.'" I could not imagine attaching a partisan label to my father's passing, or having that reaction to the news of anyone dying. But this is the world we live in, I suppose.

I also wasn't prepared for what was waiting for me in Los Angeles. I don't suppose anyone could be, even those of us who live our lives constantly in the media eye. My Los Angeles home was surrounded by media vehicles. It was a total circus, overwhelming in normal circumstances and unbearable amidst our exhaustion and grief. So we booked a room at a local hotel. My sisters and I decided to use that as a meeting place and base of operations. Both of them came by with their significant others shortly after Danielle and I checked in.

My older sister Nicole was dating a guy named Mark. My younger sister Mariann was dating a guy named Eric. My sisters were not getting along before the murder, so things were already tense and awkward. And this was the first time we had all been together in a while.

After we met to share information and to discuss coordinating communications with the investigators, I'll never forget what happened next. Each of my sisters pulled me aside separately and said some very disparaging things about each other's boyfriend, things that were troubling in their implications.

I had spent years immersed in my work and my young family, and stayed in Sacramento for most of the year. Therefore, I had remained in blissful ignorance of familial jealousies and squabbles. So the implications of these requests took me completely by surprise, and not in a pleasant way.

All of us then drove over to meet the detectives at my dad's home and tour the crime scene.

My dad's street—the street I grew up on—was small, and there was a continual media presence there since the word got out. Relatives of sitting politicians don't get murdered every day, and the crime was also tremendously shocking, both for the victim and the location. My father was a beloved senior citizen with no enemies, and he lived in the quiet Silver Lake neighborhood, an oasis of peace, with a beautiful man-made lake, in the middle of Los Angeles, just east of the Hollywood Hills.

I didn't want to talk to the media that night. I was devastated, confused, overwhelmed, exhausted, drained, sad, and perplexed—you name it. But I knew many of the reporters on site, and I respected them, and I also knew they wouldn't give up until I shared with them a few words.

I said something like, "well, might as well get this over with," and I walked to meet the cameras.

Regrets

It was during those initial brief interviews that I had some profound realizations about life. When I go back and watch those interviews, I see raw emotion. I couldn't complete many sentences without breaking down. Grief is unpleasant to experience in private. That night, I showed my grief—and perhaps some regrets— very publicly.

The hardest then (and the hardest now) is whenever something reminds me of how much more time I should have spent with my dad—and how my son will never meet him at all.

You see, when I was a kid, I almost never saw my dad. He grew up extremely deprived during the depths of the Great Depression. Both of his brothers, whose key childhood years were not during the worst of the Depression, were well over 6-foot tall. Not my dad. His family was so poor during his key formative years, that malnutrition, including rickets, had stunted his growth.

According to my dad, during those times, his father made $40 a month, and drank $35 of it. I can't say I blamed my grandfather. He came to the United States at age 19 from a verdant and bucolic mountain valley in Italy, southeast of the Amalfi Coast. He went from a quiet, green, sunny, outdoor farm life to the (vastly better-paying) job of a coal miner, spending every waking moment underground.

The conditions in those Pennsylvania coal mines were rough and unsafe. Several of his cousins had been among the 362 miners killed in West Virginia's

Monongah Mining Disaster, but he pressed on. Hearing and reading those stories had instilled in me a profound desire to fight for working people, and are one of the main reasons I ran for office.

After almost a decade as a miner, my grandfather had headed west to a Colorado boom town where he got promoted from the guy mining the coal underground, to the guy shoveling it into a furnace above ground to make steel. Despite the promotion, again I don't fault him for being miserable. Conditions then were awful. No air conditioning, no protective equipment. He used to shovel coal in a steel blast furnace for 8+ hours a day. He would lose several pounds of water weight every day at work.

Later, too old to fight in World War II, my grandfather worked for the Air Force in Oakland. He would arrive at work, build the skeleton of a miniature model city, and at the end of the day, watch the bombers blow them up for target practice. It didn't exactly give him a grand sense of accomplishment and job satisfaction, doing that every day.

As a result of growing up so wanting, my father lived his entire working life like he was being chased by the demon of childhood poverty, something he did not want to face ever again. He had all of my grandfather's work ethic, coupled with a burning desire not to be him. While my grandfather smoked and drank heavily, my father never did. (I saw him have a drink for the first time in his sixties). While my grandfather was brutish and uneducated, my father worshipped education. He earned several Master's degrees, founded the Los Angeles County High School for the Arts, became a professor, and authored several textbooks. But his fear of poverty, coupled with poor economic conditions during my first eight years of life, meant that I rarely saw my dad during much of my own formative years.

My father worked three jobs to make sure we would never starve, and to save for college tuition for his children, in an era where there was nowhere near the public and private aid we have today. Every day, he would get up at 5am, drive to his job as a teacher, plan his lessons, and work a full day. Then, he'd come home, change clothes, and go work at Dodger Stadium. He began there selling peanuts and ended up managing a concession that sold ice cream and other snacks. He worked all eighty-one Dodger home games and all the special events like concerts. With most Dodger games running from approximately 7 to 10pm, he'd get home very late, well after I was in bed. On Saturdays, he had a third job, teaching at a college of design.

On Sundays, he finally rested. We all went to church, together, but the family, sensing this was his only time all week to take a deep breath and be alone with his thoughts, gave him wide breadth. All of this meant that I maybe saw him a couple hours per week.

My father's schedule improved a little over the years, but by then I was a teenager, with a typical teen's disdain for parental involvement. I went off to college at age 17, concluding a childhood that seemed short and devoid of much fatherly presence. But then as an adult in my own work life, I became guilty of the same workaholic tendencies of my father and grandfather.

Two things had moderated those tendencies a bit: marrying Danielle, and having children myself. Each changed me. And ironically, my father was a part of it. At some point in life, I concluded that anyone who takes time out of their busy day to give you advice is someone who cares about you. This sounds obvious, but consider how few people heed advice from their elders.

Anyway, so when my dad saw me on the same awful workaholic path, especially when I started considering having children of my own, he used to look me in the eye, and say, "Michael—you gotta make sure you smell the flowers." Later, he told me how much he loved Danielle because she was the only one who had been able to get me to do so.

They say there are moments when everything comes rushing to you, and something, like the above, which takes several paragraphs to explain, is perceived—or perhaps the right word is, "felt"—in one split second. I *felt* all the above when the reporters asked me, "What was your father like growing up?" When asked that the night, I started to explain how he worked three jobs so that we would have better lives than he did, and how I would not have had the same opportunities, if he had been lazier. I felt how this made me not really see him much as a child. And how now I would never see him again. And then I started welling up and couldn't complete my thoughts.

TOURING THE CRIME SCENE

A pair of LAPD detectives and their very hardworking crew chief (who had been awake for something like 36 hours at that point) introduced themselves and escorted us around the house. They needed help to locate all of my father's electronic devices, and anything else that could be of help.

My father lived in a three-level house on a tiny, hilly street with only two other homes, both across the street. If you were facing my father's front door, here was your view: To the far left, down the hill, was the lake, and the nice jogging path around it. Looking at his home, you saw a connected, two-car garage on your right. To the left, as the home sloped down the hill, were the downstairs bedrooms.

As you entered the foyer, the garage-to-home entry door was just to your right, and to your left was a small staircase that led upstairs. On the main, middle level was a large living room, dining room, and the kitchen. Up another short staircase took you to the master suite and one smaller bedroom that my dad used for storage. My father's bedroom (the master) was built directly above the garage. The desk, where he was found murdered, was at the deepest part of the room. There was only one door to his bedroom, furthest from where his desk was.

It was hard entering the room where my father had just been killed. But we had to, to help the police. I took a deep breath and walked in. What did I notice? First, there was a large gold ring on a countertop in the room, which the burglar had not stolen. Yet, oddly, my father's small, wooden-file cabinet had been hacked open. Many electronics were still present, and had not been taken. Ditto for the art hanging on the wall, some of which was fairly valuable. Adding to the surreal vibe was the fact that many sections of the house were covered with fingerprinting dust.

On the floor near my father's desk was one tantalizing page of handwritten notes indicating that he wanted to change his will—something he had told me several times in the months leading up to his murder, but something I had not thought about until then.

AN INOPPORTUNE TIME FOR A SCOLDING

That night I also had another hard conversation, this time with the detectives, as a sidebar. My immediate concern was making sure that my father's murder wasn't politically connected, and that the rest of my family was not in danger. People tend to internalize things, and I, like any other politician, had made several enemies in my time in office. So one of the first things I asked them was whether they thought the murder might have been a message to me.

Who did I think might be behind it, during those initial confusing moments? I had two concerns. First, in my role as Chairman of the Appropriations Committee, I had recently killed a bill that would have required condoms in pornographic videos. My committee analysts thought that telling any filmmakers what they had to depict in their films was a First Amendment violation, and that passing the bill would ensure an expensive lawsuit for our cash-strapped state in the

depths of a recession. For such a silly bill, I was not
prepared for the vitriol from its backers—they were
inordinately upset. Something about their tactics
worried me. The police politely laughed at my concerns.

The year before, I had also introduced legislation to
protect male circumcision, after some very anti-Semitic
people had tried to ban it in California. This had sparked
some very over-the-top protests, from some guys who
blamed their lack of self-esteem on their lack of foreskin.
Their protests were also over-the-top, and featured lots
of fake blood and lots of threats. The police chuckled at
this too.

My third concern was that members of an ethnic
empowerment group were behind it. I had been on the
ballot six times at this point, and five of those six times,
I had by chance bested a candidate backed by this group.
Their tactics, too, were out of line, even by the standards
of modern politics. They followed my then-pregnant
wife. They stalked my staff. They threatened and they
libeled.

And my father had recently involved himself in their
affairs, reporting voter fraud they had allegedly
committed in a local council race. Don't get me wrong,
I was supported financially and electorally by every
other organization representing this ethnic group, had
wonderful relations with much of their clergy, and had
even been given the highest honor by their homeland
government. But this one local faction was violently
opposed to me and didn't feel constrained by even the
limited norms of political decorum. The police pooh-

poohed this too. Later, however, the idea resurfaced because of a very specific tip.

During the conversation, the police politely listened, but then directly reassured me, rather emphatically, that they did not believe my father's killing to be politically motivated. Their line, which I'll never forget, was, "if they wanted to object that hard, they would've just killed you."

But my questions and concerns were not the difficult part of this conversation. Instead, it was what the two detectives decided to editorialize on. They let drop that while they didn't think the murder was politically motivated, it still could have resulted indirectly from my actions as a lawmaker.

The legislation the detectives chided me about was Assembly Bill 109, which, unfortunately, like much we were asked to vote on, was OK in theory, but horrible in execution. You see, for years, people in law enforcement and people who worked to rehabilitate criminals kept noticing a pattern. Say 19-year-old Johnny Papermill, a high-school dropout from Humboldt County, living with his single mother, got convicted for marijuana dealing or some other relatively minor crime. Young and misguided Johnny would get sentenced to state prison and emerge five years later a hardened criminal.

The thought was that if Johnny could serve his time in the local Humboldt County Jail instead of state prison, he'd have more of a chance to rehabilitate. His mom could visit regularly, reproach him for his misdeeds, and cheer him on in his efforts to get an education. The kindly local sheriffs, who knew that Johnny's father had drunk himself to death when the paper mill shut down, would have a better understanding of his circumstances, an understanding that can only come from a strong sense of community.

All this, plus the very needy condition of the state budget, made Governor Jerry Brown push AB 109, which he labeled with the somewhat Orwellian term, "Re-Alignment."

The above was the *theory* behind the bill. But AB 109 was horrible in *fact*. In a few small counties in California, it probably worked OK. In small rural communities, the above example was probably fairly true to reality. However, much of California's population lives in the large counties: Los Angeles, San Francisco, and Alameda. And in those counties, AB 109 was a disaster.

In those counties, some *already* hardened criminal would get sentenced to state prison. He'd then get "realigned" to county jail. The county jail system in big counties was no better equipped to rehabilitate that young man, and in many cases, it was worse. But most significantly, the jails in the larger counties were overcrowded and under (or soon to be under) court orders to lessen that overcrowding. Thus, AB 109, coupled with other laws or decrees, simply just forced county officials to turn criminals loose early.

In other words—in the major urban counties, AB 109 used the theory of Johnny Papermill to take someone convicted of a serious crime—a crime that previously merited a stint in state prison—to be transferred to county jail, where, because of overcrowding, that person would simply be let free.

The detectives *could not help themselves* from using this opportunity to scold the legislature for passing it and me for voting on it. I felt terrible.

If their comments sound harsh, unprofessional, and ill-timed, it's because they were. As I learned over the course of the relationship, one of the two detectives didn't have a great bedside manner. I thought it was wrong to spit out political invective—which, believe me he did—to a grieving son of a murder victim. Nevertheless, when I tell this story—and it took me a long time to tell it—I give it as an example to always trust your heart as a legislator, and to remember that votes always have consequences.

AB 109 was the hardest vote I had taken up to that point. Indeed, I had planned to vote "no", but Governor Brown and the legislative leadership employed a nasty tactic. They made AB 109 part of the budget.

There is an unwritten rule in the California legislature that members of the majority party do not vote against the budget. Those who did had seen their committee chairs stripped, their bills die, and had even been transferred into offices so small that their staff could not fit—all for voting against the budget. In 2011, it just didn't happen. So by making AB 109 a budget "trailer bill," the proponents all but ensured its fate.

Lots of people don't understand why lawmakers don't do the pure thing on every issue. They don't understand that a legislative body is all about tradeoffs. Imagine you got elected to the legislature a couple generations ago. You ran for office because your cousin perished in a horrible car accident, and since then, you made it your life's mission to reform car-safety laws. You want to take the radical step of requiring things like seat belts and airbags, and prohibiting people from driving drunk. What people don't grasp is that ideas don't progress in a vacuum. Sadly, they don't even progress based on merit. In a legislature, ideas become reality based on the relationships and power of their proponents.

Let's say now, that after ten years of fighting the automotive industry, your big seatbelt bill will finally come up for a hearing, and you think you have the votes. You know that this bill will save millions of lives, and likely would have saved your cousin's family immeasurable grief. The bill is going to be heard in Chairman Jones' committee on Tuesday. Like some in politics, Chairman Jones is a petty, vindictive SOB, and he's expressed lukewarm support of your bill, but his support or opposition will clearly make the difference.

On Monday, Chairman Jones' bill, which is going to tax the pretty ribbons worn on the dresses of orphan schoolgirls, comes up for a vote. It's a dumb bill, and you're not too happy about taking money from these poor young ladies.

Do you vote against it?

These are the tradeoffs lawmakers must make all the time. I submit, if you truly believe your automotive-safety legislation will save lives, you probably hold your nose and vote to tax the orphans' ribbons.

A similar scenario comes up another way often. Let's say your same seatbelt bill is set for a vote, and the only reason it survived this session is because you got appointed to chair a powerful committee. Fearing your power, your colleagues are finally willing to buck the powerful lobby that has killed any meaningful reforms for decades.

Now the house leader, who appointed your chair (and can just as easily remove you) asks for your vote on Jones' stupid ribbon tax. What do you say?

This is the nuance of life as a lawmaker. Is it great? No. It feels pretty awful at times. But if you believe in yourself and the ideas you wish to advance, there are tradeoffs you make.

None of this is say that my vote on AB 109 was the right one. I had misgivings even at the time, without the benefit of hindsight or the knowledge of how big-county sheriffs would execute it. It was a big enough vote that you could argue that concern should have trumped every other consideration.

But putting all that aside, here's where I come down: My gut told me not to vote for AB 109. And in politics, you have to trust your gut. I should never have voted for it.

Did that make it right for the detectives to tell me at that moment that my vote led to my father's murder? I'll let you decide. I can tell you that in life, timing is everything. A suggestion that lawmakers more carefully consider the consequences of their votes would probably have been appropriate at a better time than twenty-four hours after I learned my father was murdered. And, as I learned later, the detectives' statement was objectively false, and they knew it.

Still, I lived the rest of my tenure in office with the philosophy of trusting my gut (or my heart). I voted no on more and more things. Year after year, I had by far the most "no" votes of any Democratic lawmaker in California. Some say this made me a "centrist." Some called me a DINO (Democrat In Name Only) and some special-interest groups attacked me. But I survived. Don't get me wrong: I was scarred. I lost some political power for sure. But I knew I could hold my head up high. My courage begat similar courage from my colleagues, ushering in a brief period, from 2014 through 2016, where common-sense predominated. And I was trusting my heart, so that hopefully I would never be in the position again to regret voting for something I sensed was wrong.

THE FIRST TANTALIZING LEADS

Readers who studied art history know that in the art world, an "icon" does not refer to Marilyn Monroe.

An icon is a kind of painting, common in Eastern Orthodox lands, that depicts a Christian religious scene on a piece of wood, often with gold or silver overlaid on parts of the paint. Originally part of Greek Orthodox culture, the first ones were painted in the Byzantine Empire, and later in the Russian Empire, which is why many people often refer to them as, "Russian icons." The typical one portrays a saint, or the virgin Mary, with real gold used to make the halo. The fact that the "canvas" is a flat piece of (now ancient) wood makes them look crude and rustic, in a cool way. Genuine icons, from certain periods centuries ago, which were acquired before the fall of the Soviet Union (and widespread fakery) are quite valuable. My father had a vast collection of such icons.

A few days before he was murdered, some local antiquarian society had advertised with fanfare something like, "on November 15, Mr. Joseph Gatto of Silver Lake will be giving a presentation on Russian icons. He'll bring to the lecture several rare and special pieces from his own collection…"

Aware of this advertisement, in the initial interviews with the media, my father's neighbors had speculated that he was killed by art thieves, who assumed his collection would be momentarily taken out of storage for his coming lecture. The word, "Russian" in the coverage connoted Russian Mafia, or some other pre-planned hit by an organized ring.

There isn't much in this book that I can rule out conclusively (OK, perhaps the foreskin militants), but I (and the police) feel fairly comfortable ruling out a Russian-icon connection. Why? Well, they found all of my father's collection still present in my father's home. Even the ones prominently displayed had not been taken. And the other clues just don't point to something like that. But for the first day, this was the only clue we had.

THE FIRST REAL CLUES

A couple days after my father's murder, some other leads began filtering in. A local mother sent around a group e-mail that on the evening of November 12, she was driving her son home from karate, when she encountered a young man, quite brazenly breaking into cars around 6:40pm. She summoned a neighbor man, who she knew. When confronted, the car burglar calmly backed away toward some community stairs.

The easiest way to conceptualize the Silver Lake neighborhood where my dad lived, is as a football stadium. The lake, on the flat part, would be the playing field. Ringing the playing field are different levels. Those levels are the conventional car streets. Connecting the car streets like the stadium aisles or tunnels were a few small, perpendicular hill streets like my dad's, but also some "walk streets" or "stair streets" or "cut throughs." (We always called them, "community stairs" growing up.)

Anyway, this woman encountered the car burglar a couple street levels above my dad's house. He headed down the community stairs, in the general direction of my father's street. The woman and a male neighbor gave chase by car, but he got away. The woman claimed that he had brandished a gun before fleeing, and described his clothing (nice but still edgy) and gear (backpack, etc.) in great detail. She stated she believed this had something to do with my father's murder.

A few days later, someone in the LAPD leaked to my sister Mariann that they had DNA evidence, but an incredibly minute bit of it. My sister initially understood the DNA to be from "a sweat droplet", but I later learned it was epithelial DNA—a few skin cells that rubbed off on certain tools at the scene.

During those first few days, I had many conversations with the detectives, and this led to more details, and even more questions.

I was not sure if this car burglar was related, nor was I sure that DNA on the tools came from the perpetrator, or even whether the perpetrator had acted alone. I preferred to work with certainties.

And this much was certain:

(1) The sun went down at 4:51pm that day, according to almanacs, as in 2013, November 12 fell during standard time.

(2) At 6:07 pm on November 12, my father was seen on video leaving the Los Feliz Costco, in the same clothes he was wearing at the time of his death. The

Costco was about fifteen minutes from my father's home, even with traffic.

(3) By 6:16 pm, again according to almanacs, the last glimmers of sun were gone that day, and it was more or less totally dark.

(4) The last activity on my dad's computer was at 7:37pm that evening. Apparently this was e-mail activity, and/or activity editing his website. However, it was not clear to me whether these were automatic actions (like a page reloading, etc.) or whether, of course, it was even my father even operating the mouse. But it is most likely that he was still alive as of 7:37pm on November 12, assuming the relevant computer clocks were set correctly.

The conversations with the police in those early days were a mix of questions from them, and questions from me. For example, they asked me whether my dad was the type of guy who sometimes put on the same clothes the next day that he had worn the previous day. I said, "sometimes", which is accurate. This told me they weren't sure whether he was killed on the 12th or 13th. However, it was much more likely to be the 12th, they said.

They asked me whether my father owned a gun. I did not know. I vaguely remember him owning one when I was a kid, which he had inherited from his father.

They asked me things like whether my father ever met ladies online. I didn't think he did, but would not be surprised, as he was fairly tech savvy (and open to dating) despite his advanced age.

Because there had been some aspersions cast by my sisters on each other's boyfriends, they also asked everyone in the family to provide a DNA sample and their phone records. This, I found almost pointless. I couldn't imagine a smart person doing a deed like this themselves. And if someone hired someone—they'd have to be monumentally stupid to make a phone call or send a text message right after the deed was done. But I provided my phone records, even though I worried they could become a curiosity to the media. Reporters love to know who lawmakers talked with before the passage of a key bill, or for that matter, what lawmakers said to (or about!) each other in text messages. This gave me a little heartburn, but of course, I provided my phone records without delay, to encourage everyone else in the family to do so as well.

THE MOST HEARTBREAKING CONVERSATION

My eldest daughter Elliana adored my dad. She was always super close with me too, one of those kids who just prefers the parent of the opposite gender. For the first several years of her life, she would only fall asleep fast if I held her—which made my travel schedule all the more guilt-inducing on me. I think she thought of my father as an older version of me. At age three, she had both of us wrapped around her finger. This was a kid who spoke in complete sentences by her first birthday. She had long, detailed conversations with him, about everything from fairies to butterflies, and he loved it.

I'll never forget when I saw my father the happiest. He had come to visit us in Sacramento, and at some point (I forget if he was coming or going), he picked her up, and Danielle said, "Elliana, give your gramps a kiss." He kind of turned his cheek, preparing for the standard little kid peck. But Elliana wasn't having it. She grabbed him by the face with two hands, and planted a giant kiss right on his smacker. At first, he was kind of shocked, kind of laughing, but then he got this immense smile on his face. His granddaughter loved him with the intensity and abandon that only childhood affords. And he was smitten too.

Every time they hung out, he would teach her to paint. He was elated that someone in the family inherited some artistic skills—as my artistic ability stunted somewhere near the "Cro-Magnon Cave Painting" level. And Elliana loved learning from him.

Anyway, at three and a half, Elliana was (like she is now), an intuitive, sensitive, intelligent kid. She knew something was wrong, but we had thus far refrained from telling her. I don't even think she understood at that time the concept of death.

Shielding her, however, proved difficult, as stories were on the radio and nightly news, and I had dozens of phone conversations every day, often in cramped quarters or a car. At some point, she overheard something. "Dad, did someone kill gramps?" My heart broke in a million pieces. We had to explain that someone gave him a "big ouchie"—so big that he wasn't coming back. I still remember how red the eyes were from the crying that night, hers and mine.

Again, death is part of life. But that doesn't make it easy to explain a murder to a young child.

LIFE HAPPENS

My "auntie" (actually, my father's first cousin) turned 80 a few days after my dad's passing. The family decided to go ahead with a (very subdued) party, at my urging, as you only turn 80 once. My sisters did not attend, as besides not being close with one another, they were also not close with most of the extended family. For me though, it was a comfort to see my cousins, including several with whom my father was really close.

However, when it rains, it pours. Unbeknownst to us of course, the restaurant had an E. Coli outbreak that day. All of us who ate the salad became violently ill—the sickest one can get, when it comes to the GI system.

I had to go on with my duties in LA, doing stuff for my constituents, and the police, and the estate. On November 19, Danielle, weak from vomiting for a day straight, collapsed and hit her head in our Sacramento house, where she had returned with our kids. A neighbor had thankfully come by to check on her, but the exertion of walking to the door caused Danielle to pass out. Our neighbor helped Danielle, and fed our children who was crying beside her. These days were very hard on us, but they were made a little easier by the people like our neighbor who helped us hold our lives together as best as we could.

When I look back on those days, not just the days right after the murder, but the years of busy days and sleepless nights that ensued, I feel bad—bad for not being there enough for Danielle and the baby. My father loved Danielle so much, and not just because he was a gentleman in the sense of the 1953 film. I remember him telling me once, "Michael, she has everything: brains, looks, ethics—and the grace and poise of Princess Diana!" This was the highest compliment he could give. The two even hung out together when I had to work—having endless discussions about this and that, and how to make the best Italian meals. So it was ironic, and not in a good way, that my dad's murder took so much time and took me away from her so much.

MORE AWKWARDNESS
FROM THE DETECTIVE

A couple weeks after my father's murder, I suggested they chat with my father's elderly first cousin, who spoke with often, and knew him and his patterns well. The detectives had already seen her name in his call logs.

"Ah, _____," one detective growled, repeating her somewhat unique Italian surname. Is that the same family as _____? Are you related to _____ _____?"

We were talking about my father's mother's family. The entire extended family gets together once a month, and has done so since the family immigrated to the United States over a hundred years ago. My dad often spoke with his first cousins, and I often spoke with my second cousins, the next generation. Having no male siblings, those male cousins are the closest thing I have to brothers.

"Yes, I replied. _____ happens to be my second cousin."

"He's a fucking asshole" the detective spat out, furious. "A real fucking dirtbag," he continued. "Fuck him."

"OK," I'm thinking. "What does that have to do with me?"

Putting aside his unprofessionalism, I was curious. My cousin lived one county over, owned a flower shop, and was the kind of guy who rode a bicycle to the beach every day in flip flops. He was older than me, and in a long-term relationship for years. Did he have some kind of criminal record in Los Angeles of which no one knew? I sincerely doubted it. So why was this LAPD detective interrupting our important discussion to crap on him?

So I asked the detective—what did my cousin do? It turns out they had attended high school together, some 30+ years previously. My cousin had briefly dated the detective's sister, and it didn't end well. All of this happened when they were 15 or 16 years old, when I was 7 or 8.

If I was a detective, I could not imagine raising this issue with such rage to the family member of a murder victim. It was random and childish to say the least. If my second cousin broke someone's heart thirty years ago, it was no fault of my father's. Needless to say, it was a strange conversation.

THE PRIMARY LEAD

On November 19, the police publicized a sketch of the young man who was seen burglarizing cars—a person of interest. Although we didn't know it at the time, that sketch would (probably incorrectly) come to dominate the investigation. The sketch depicted what could at best be described as an amorphous or generic young Caucasian or Hispanic man. As I'll explain, I spent so much time focused on that sketch: poring over yearbook photos—studying the faces of every vagrant—begging the public for help to find him. If I knew at the time the details surrounding the sketch, I might have behaved differently.

CLEFTS

By November 20, taxed by the constant stress, the tensions that existed in our family surfaced. I felt like both sisters, perhaps spurred on by their significant others, had shown signs of greed. To me, negotiating the financial minefields of my father's estate felt like a distinctly secondary task, to be addressed only after getting some answers in the investigation into my father's death. But I was perhaps in better shape financially than they were, so I tried not to judge.

I also felt a deep sense of ironic melancholy. A death can bring a family together, or it can tear them further apart. I loved my family. We had grown up together during tough economic times. Life wasn't always easy. My parents didn't always get along. My younger sister got pregnant at age 14. We didn't always have the material things that others had. But we had been very close at times, stepping up to help one another with everything from getting through college to raising a child. And my father wanted nothing more than for us siblings to get along. He'd smile down upon us from heaven, if we had found a way to do so after he left us. But that was not to be. The siblings lawyered up, and started to bicker over aspects of my father's estate – the last thing we needed with the crime still unsolved.

THE FUNERAL

I've given a lot of speeches in my life. Surely the most difficult one I ever had to give was my father's eulogy, November 25. Given everything going on, I hadn't had a chance to process much. And the funeral turned very much into a public spectacle, with over 1000 mourners, many of them who I knew from politics, packing into our church that holds about 250.

I had grown up in that parish, attending elementary school there, and serving as an altar boy for much of my childhood. The last time I had been up on that altar was baptizing my nephew and godson Damian, who my sister Mariann had had at age 15. The time before that, it had been as an altar boy.

My father had grown more devout in his later years—or perhaps more sad. Our parish priest confided in me that my father went through some periods where he attended church every day—and sat there in what appeared to be melancholy contemplation. When I heard that, I immediately understood how sad he had been that certain family members weren't getting along. I had seen that look in my father's eyes in church before, when as a young man, the peace and quiet of church was the only time in the week when he wasn't working, and often the only time he was with his family.

All of these things were on my mind that day. I also had to be strong for my family and for the people coming to mourn my father. I had to greet the many guests, who had shown up to pay their respects—from the Speaker of the State Assembly, to the Mayor of Los Angeles, to the Primate of the Western Diocese of the Armenian church, whose presence meant a lot to me. And I had to try to express what my father meant to me and to so many others. This is what I said:

Wow. I think the last time I was up here in front of so many people, I was an altar boy at Midnight Mass, trying to stay awake. Now I stand here before you, at my father's funeral, trying to keep my composure.

I think most of you know the basic outline of my father's life, so I will focus on Joe Gatto the man. For those of you who don't know his story, here it is, briefly: He was born five years into the Great Depression, in Pueblo, Colorado. After the family moved to Los Angeles, my father attended Fairfax High School. He lettered in four sports, on teams that were the stuff of legend, and many of his teammates went on to play professional ball.

My father joined the Army, and then traveled the world—and I mean, the entire world—in the 1960s. He could tell stories of having to swat a thousand flies off his lunch in some alley in Cairo. But when he returned, he settled down, had three children, and began teaching. And boy could he teach. He was honored by two Presidents and several legislatures. He co-founded Los Angeles' original Arts High School, the LA County High School for the Arts. In the days since my father's death, so many of his students have come forward and talked about how he changed their lives.

I'd like to ask something: would anyone who was a student of my father please stand up?

Look around, this was a great teacher. And since the books my father wrote were used as textbooks from Canada to Texas, I am sure he touched the lives of people he didn't even teach in person.

When my dad retired, he pursued other things: with a little help, he was elected as a delegate to the Democratic National Committee, and got to attend two national conventions, a longtime goal of his. And he—finally— was able to pursue his lifelong passion, which was making art. He died at the peak of his success, as his jewelry was beginning to attract major attention and win major awards.

He loved gardening, was a knowledgeable collector, and a doting grandfather.

That is his biographical sketch. It is a testament to his qualities, that so many of you, from different stages of his life, are here today. Now let's talk about Joe Gatto the man.

Over the last week, I've asked many of you to help me in describing him. The picture that has emerged was sometimes touching, sometimes compelling, and often pretty darn funny.

Here is the summary: Joe Gatto was a man with strong and unique ideals, who gave tough love, and loved his heritage. He was incredibly hard-working, had Depression values but a great sense of adventure, and he could be stubborn. He was ageless, timeless, and possessed a deep love for his family.

Of the billions of souls that preceded us on Earth, and the billions that will doubtlessly follow, all of us in this room were lucky to have crossed paths with him, if even for a few moments.

Let's talk about his unique values and ideas. Now some of you folks have had the misfortune of playing Trivial Pursuit with me. And you've wondered why I usually get five pie pieces in one long extended roll, but then I always have a real hard time getting that last pop-culture pie piece? Well that's because of my dad. See, for most of our childhood, he raised us without television or movies of any kind. How uh, strict was this upbringing? Well, when I met Danielle, I had to explain to her why an Italian who loves boxing, loves running, and loves working out hadn't seen Rocky.

And when people say things to me, like, "may the force be with you," I would often just stare back blankly. Oh how we hated this as a kid! But when I attended law school, my Professors said I had this focus that was not typical for the modern generation. I credit that to my dad.

Since his death, I've really enjoyed hearing his students and neighbors talk about him, and I've been *amused at how the stories are split between "he was the most peaceful man in the world," and "his love was a tough love." For what it's worth, I come down on the latter side.*

Now I'm not saying it wasn't effective. When we kids were growing up, we went through a messy phase and ground zero was my bedroom. Somewhere out there I see my staff and my wife expressing shock. But it's true: I wasn't always so anal retentive, and I really did go through a messy phase. And my dad's solution was amusing. He told me that in the Army, your room had to be so clean it would pass the White Glove test, and your bed made so tight, you could bounce a quarter off of it. He then proceeded to strip my bed of its bedding and put on it his old Army blankets. And then he marched into my room for the next few days, with a white glove and a quarter to test both. I can still picture him bouncing that quarter off my bed. I've been extremely organized ever since.

My father loved his heritage. He would travel to Italy every three years or so, re-taught himself the language, and tried (mostly unsuccessfully) to cook good Italian food.

Now although he loved all women, and particularly those from the colder climes, he really loved being Southern Italian. Any weakness in any of the three kids, he attributed to our partial Northern European ancestry. One time, I broke my arm in a motorcycle accident, and he attributed it, of course, to my non-Italian blood. He kind of waived his oversized wrists and then looked at my cast and said, "Yeah, that's that Northern blood," . . . "it'll thin ya out."

One thing for sure about my dad, is he was hardworking. My friends in high school called him "The Ox." When he was a kid, he'd get up early and sell papers. When he was a teen, he worked as a bag boy at a grocery store. During most of my childhood, we worked three jobs. Two teaching jobs, one during the day, and one on the weekend. And at night, he worked at Dodger Stadium.

I want you to imagine his life. Getting up each day at 5 am, going to work a full day teaching, and then coming home briefly to change clothes, and drive somewhere else to do it all again, often until 10 pm at night or later.

Despite this grueling schedule, when he retired, we were told he hadn't missed a day of work for his entire career, which spanned over 40 years.

When we asked my dad if this was true, he said, "aw heck, the streak is longer than that. I haven't missed a day of school since the 4th Grade."

One thing I will miss the most is his Depression values, something he passed along to me, and his boyish sense of adventure. Both were on display whenever he came to visit us at our Sacramento abode. You see, where we stay in Sacramento was built on an old farm. But the developers left the old trees, and coming up to visit would just drive my father crazy—just nuts—that none of our neighbors picked their fruit. So he and I would go around the neighborhood and steal it: we'd come home with persimmons, pomegranates, oranges, apples, jujubes—you name it.

But our funniest adventure by far happened just three weeks ago, and had to do with olives. Every year, I cure the olives that no one picks, and this year—he and I decided that we would expand and make olive oil too. So we went around and picked pound after pound of olives. And then we crushed them, we food processed them (and poor Danielle was watching us make this huge mess) and we used an old t-shirt to squeeze the oil out of the pulp. Well . . . What we got from all those pounds of olives, was this . . . goo. I mean, we got one beaker of a tricolor liquid, where the top layer, maybe half an inch tall max, was oil. I put a picture of it up on Facebook, and no one could guess what the heck it was.

My father could be stubborn, that's for sure. Other Italians use the word "testadura" to describe folks from our region of origin. It means hard-headed, but it also means, "dogged" or "determined." But with my dad, just plain "stubborn" seemed to fit. In 1989, our whole family took this epic trip to Europe. We did like seven countries in three weeks. For the first part of the trip, my mom was still at home with one kid, so my dad had to make do on his own, with two others. One time, we got on this train in Germany with the goal of getting to Austria, Salzburg or something. Anyway, I forget exactly what happened, but there was some kind of debate about whether we were on the proper train or not, and whether it was headed in the right direction, and the debate involved at least three *languages. Anyway, because of my dad's stubbornness, I got to see France.*

My dad's stubbornness was part of his refusal to slow down. This was a constant source of anxiety but also mirth for the family. We came to his house a couple years ago and watched with open mouths as he moved a tree with a huge root ball, by wrapping it in a burlap sack and hauling it around the yard into another five-foot hole he had personally dug. Another time we caught him dead lifting a small refrigerator. This was a man in his late seventies, you understand. And he had no idea.

And living until age 78 is certainly a long life by most measures, but Joe Gatto almost reaching 80 does not compensate for the rage we feel for him being taken from us early. A few years back, we took one of those home ancestry tests, and it showed that we bear that Centenarian gene that you may have seen on Oprah.

So we honestly thought he would be with us another twenty or 25 years.

In the immediate future, many of you have noted how upsetting it will be that he will not be there to walk Mariann down the aisle next May when she marries Eric. In the long term, I can tell you that I am also upset that he will not be there to see Damian graduate college or to see my daughters graduate high school or get married, because we honestly thought he would be.

We knew he would be there, because he was so proud of his grandchildren. Now close your ears, Danielle, but like me, my dad wanted us to have ten kids. On the day I learned that Danielle was pregnant with Evie, she didn't tell me: I came home, and Elliana was wearing a shirt that said "big sister." So, continuing the same theme, we casually e-mailed a picture of Elliana wearing the shirt to my dad, and at first he didn't notice. But when he did, it was hard to tell who was more excited, me or him!

Dad's love for his grandchildren was unconditional love, infinite love. And it flowed both ways. Damian has lost his friend, his mentor, and a father figure. May the lessons he taught you Damian live on, as long as you draw breath, and may you pass them on to your children someday.

Of my children, only Elliana really got to know her grandfather. But each of them will miss him so much, and he will miss so much. On the day after we heard the news, my daughter Evie stood up for the first time. Last week, she took her first tentative steps. We are so sad that he will not be around to get to know her, and vice versa. But we are and will remain thankful for the time he did get, with his other grandkids, Elliana, and Damian.

I think I speak for everyone present when I say that our hearts are broken. We are struggling mightily to understand the dark nature of certain human souls.

Deaths like my father's are particularly difficult, because none of us got a chance to say "goodbye." No words can express our grief, no platitudes can assuage our sense of loss, and times like this rightfully shake the very foundations of our faith.

But it is up to us, the living, despite our sense of profound unfairness, to rise each day and take from Joe Gatto's life all the wonderful lessons we can learn.

Celebrate life like he did, every minute, every day. Put your family first. Spend time enjoying the intangible and profound: conversations, travel, art. Cherish your time on this earth, and protect it always.

An idealistic, tough-loving teacher, who loved his heritage, worked incredibly hard, wasted nothing, collected everything, and above all, loved his family. These are the qualities that were Joe Gatto.

And may we be so lucky that they describe each of us some day.

May we never forget the traits we valued in him, and may we never forget the special memories we have of Joe Gatto.

I choked up or broke down momentarily a few times during the speech. The first time, I think, was when I asked his former students to stand up—and HUNDREDS of people, ranging in age from their thirties to their sixties, slowly rose *en masse*. The other times were when I spoke about him not being able to be there around my kids—because I know that my father loved them so much.

MORE FAILED EFFORTS

In early December 2013, the police issued a bulletin seeking jewelry made by my father. To recap, they believe that while the perpetrator didn't get at most of his jewelry, the perpetrator did apparently get away with some. So, the police asked newspapers to help them spread the word for pawn shops and similar establishments (which they also contacted directly) to be on the lookout for my father's jewelry—which was intensely unique, and hallmarked (signed) by him. However, I want to stress that my father's jewelry was made of silver, occasionally gold, and artistic elements from around the world that he incorporated into it. In other words, the raw value of each piece was in the hundreds, not thousands of dollars. It was his artistic talent that made them sell for more. He never made anything with diamonds and platinum.

This was another area where my father's lack of organization and the disorganized and slow approach to his estate probably hurt us. Did my father somewhere keep a log of all of his pieces? Likely. Could we, with enough resources, match all the jewelry pieces that remained in his house with that list, to determine exactly which might have been taken, and what they looked like? Likely. But this was never done, so police and I were forced to speculate, and show general pictures of my father's designs.

As with other leads and ideas—nothing usable came out of this. To the best of my knowledge, not a single piece of stolen jewelry has ever turned up.

LIFE LESSONS FROM THE FUNERAL

You can learn a lot about how people handle other people's moments of need. When I was running for office, almost all of my friends and most of the people I had dated—knowing that a campaign for California state office in a district with 500,000 people was an undertaking of some magnitude that I had long planned for—came in and volunteered for my campaign. By doing so, they showed that they were intellectually and ethically consistent. If they cared about me before, they still cared about me enough to help in my moment of need.

But two of my ex-girlfriends who lived in my district—ironically, the two who claimed to love me the most when I was with them—put up lawn signs for my opponents. And they didn't even know each other or my opponent!

Running for office also had brought out some strange requests from previously close friends. One friend demanded I find him a no-show patronage job, using my position. I thought he watched too much TV! Such jobs don't really exist anymore, and I tried to explain that to him, gently mentioning the obvious morality issue too.

Anyway, I always thought that some component of friendship and love is forever, and that it's best not to try to actively hurt people you once care about. Whether others shared these principles was tested at my dad's funeral, an intense moment of need for me.

Remember, my father's slaying was front-page news all across California and much of the U.S. I was contacted by people I hadn't heard from since college, who lived in the wilderness of Maine, who had heard the news and wanted to send condolences. Most of the people whose lives I had touched attended my dad's funeral or sent a card. To me, this simple gallant act was a way to say, "we care about you enough to be present and to express sympathy but we're not so focused on our past that we'll walk past you on the roadside of grief." I suppose even if they were still not over things, their attendance meant they would put aside their emotions to be present when it mattered—a very adult behavior.

That is, everyone except the lawn-sign exes and the patronage-job friend. I found it ironic and a little funny. Two of them had been close to my father. One of them had told me adamantly that she loved me more than life itself, and that we were going to spend the rest of our lives together.

These insights led me to use the funeral, in part subconsciously, as a litmus test of whether someone was decent enough to remain in my life. And it made me realize why older guys, the traditionalists, in everything from CEO to crime-boss movies, always tell their underlings, "you show up to the damn funeral."

PATTERNS? OR NOT.

In late December 2013, the San Gabriel Valley Tribune reported that detectives were looking into a spate of home-invasion robberies in Los Angeles County. The article's author cited my father's case, and a bunch of other high-profile home invasions that had occurred. To me, this evidenced the difficulty of trying to discern patterns in crime. How many home-invasions occur in any given month in a populous urban county like Los Angeles? A lot. Most involve people followed home from casinos or cash businesses.

Given the circumstances of my father's case, I highly doubt this crime followed the typology in the category, although I suppose it cannot be ruled out as a possibility.

Another concept a law-enforcement friend reminded me of was called, "don't read the crime blotter." In the heyday of the newspaper era, most local newspapers carried a column called the crime blotter, where it would detail all the crimes committed in a locale during a given week. Someone reading it would often get the impression that even very safe neighborhoods were quite dangerous. In my father's case, his point was: at any given two-hour time frame in Los Angeles, someone within a two-mile radius is breaking into a car. Thus, we shouldn't necessarily assume the car burglar was our suspect.

When I inquired about this concept to the detectives working my father's case, one said, "when I see a horse running by, I don't go looking for no unicorn." They seemed convinced that the car burglar was relevant.

To summarize:

• On one hand you have the dual concepts that "patterns" can be elusive. In urban areas like Los Angeles, there are always home-invasions and auto break-ins occurring. It is a mistake to assume they are related. If you scrutinize any moment in time too hard, in a search for meaning (as study after study has documented with the Kennedy assassination), you find false patterns.

• On the other hand, you have the principle of "Occam's razor." The simplest explanation is usually the right one. If a guy is running around the neighborhood with a gun, and then someone turns up dead, it's likely that person had something to do with it.

I'm not sure which is right.

THE EMERGING CONSENSUS

During those first few months after my father's murder, I spoke very often with the LAPD. And the media. And the community. It slowly became clear to me that a narrative had emerged about what had happened. Mind you, nobody really knew anything. Even the most informed detectives were operating on a lot of assumptions—which is natural because there was such a vacuum. But a clear consensus was emerging.

The consensus went as follows: There was a young man breaking into cars about a quarter mile from my dad's house, sometime in the second half of the 6 o'clock hour. He likely had a gun and was threatening. Locals gave chase. He likely knew the neighborhood well, because he knew where the somewhat hidden staircases were. (To outsiders, those staircases looked like they led to people's homes).

The car burglar turned right after running down the stairs, because that is what right-handed people do. He ran down my dad's street to hide, because it looked very quiet, perhaps like an alley to him.

At that moment, a tour helicopter flew overhead, taking tourists to the Hollywood sign. But he thought it was an LAPD chopper. So he thought he had to get indoors.

At that precise moment, my dad came downstairs to get his printer out of his car. He had to open the back door of his car (a hatchback) to do so, because it wouldn't fit through the side doors of his car. To open the hatchback, he had to open the garage door. As he struggled with the printer upstairs and closed the garage door, the young man ducked under it to hide from the chopper.

The young man sat in the garage for about an hour, while my dad tooled around on his computer. At some point, desperate for a fix, he went into the house. He confronted my dad, perhaps to rob him, and the gun went off, likely accidentally.

He watched my father bleed to death. High on drugs, he then tried to break into my dad's safes with garden shears and a fireplace poker. Unable to do so, he partially ransacked the room, breaking open a file cabinet, and taking a few pieces of jewelry and maybe some cash from my father's wallet (but not his credit cards). He then ran off with the items in his backpack, and got away.

None of the thousands of joggers who use the 2.5-mile track around Silver Lake saw him.

This is the story the police told me, one the media accepted, and one the public was asked to help with. And I dutifully circulated as wide as possible the sketch of the car burglar, asking the public for help.

SO MANY QUESTIONS

All the above made sense, but only if you were willing to accept that my father was the victim of truly awful timing, and that the perpetrator was high on drugs.

First the awful timing. Talk about wrong place, wrong time. My father goes downstairs to fetch his newly bought printer. He has to open the garage door when he finds it doesn't fit out the side doors of his car. At that moment, some kind of helicopter flies overhead, so the guy decides to duck under the garage door. All of these things had to fall in place exactly for this theory to work.

The "high on drugs" part makes sense if you consider all the strange things the perpetrator did. And would in theory explain all the inconsistencies in the story.

I had so many questions:

- Why would car burglar be packing a gun? It's not typical. Usually those who break into cars do so unarmed, because a petty theft charge usually means no time in jail, whereas doing so armed usually means a year or more. You simply don't need a gun to break into cars.

- Why would he be breaking into cars at a time when people were coming home from work, on a lit street, with barking dogs? I mean, even the quietest residential streets are virtual beehives of activity during the hour when people are returning from work. So it was a VERY odd time to be breaking into cars—unless you *wanted* to be noticed?

- If the witnesses were so sure they saw a gun— why on earth would they follow him?

- The staircase he fled down leads directly to a short street straight on, that leads directly to the busy street where one could get away. Why did the car burglar turn right instead, and then left down my dad's street, instead of heading directly to an easy getaway?

- How did the car burglar get into the house? Did he really have the extraordinary timing to duck under the garage door? And if my dad had accidentally left the garage door open, who closed it?

- Why would ANYONE choose to enter a house with three cars parked in front—two in the garage and one in the driveway? This is important. It was dark already and lights were surely on in my dad's house. (He was working upstairs and always kept lights on downstairs). With three cars in the driveway and lights on, a stranger wouldn't know if the Ukrainian Sniper's Club was over for a visit, or if this was a family consisting of two seven-foot-tall wrestlers. Entering such a house with three cars present was odd.

- Why would a thief not steal items from the garage and simply take off? It was filled with valuable tools and such.

- Why would a car burglar seek the only inhabited part of the house, the third floor, where for all he knew, people were present?

- Why would anyone try to break into a safe with ridiculous tools? My dad owned those old-fashioned safes, about waist height, with immensely thick walls. The burglar made an effort (or perhaps a spectacle or a show?) of trying to break into the safe with the equivalent of large scissors—the tools you use to trim a light hedge.

- How did he get away? Did he have help, or a getaway car? Of the hundreds of joggers, most of whom saw the subsequent press coverage—no one saw a guy running down the street with a backpack?

- There were unidentified prints inside my dad's house. How is it that they didn't match prints on the car? For that matter, were there any unidentified prints on the car?

- If the burglar was truly a druggie looking for a fix, which explains all the other inconsistencies and stupid behaviors, why not just hold someone up? He had a gun, allegedly. For that matter, why not trade his gun for drugs—which is common for those in need of a fix?

We've all seen those crime dramas where someone works as a criminal profiler. Profiling the killer here was so important to getting some answers and pointing things in the right direction. So I kept pressing the police for details about the crime scene and the investigation.

Over the course of several conversations with the investigators during the months after the murder, I learned things like the fact that the killer had left the gun's spent cartridge behind. That he had apparently taken cash from my dad's wallet but no credit cards. That the police's investigation of telephone towers nearby had yielded no real leads. And that the checks stolen from the car on the nearby street had never been cashed.

While I desperately wanted to be able to profile the killer, doing so had just produced another roster of inconsistencies. Any way you looked at the evidence, there was just no way to resolve those inconsistences.

I separated what we knew about the killer's actions (and the car thief's) into several broad categories.

Certain reconstructed or assumed actions made him appear bold, brazen, desperate, or gutsy. For example, entering what might have appeared to have been an occupied house. Burglarizing cars at an hour when people are coming home from work. Waiving a gun at people. Perhaps not freaking out after the gunshot. Not wearing gloves. Packing a gun for a car burglary. These are the actions of someone who is audacious and brazen.

Certain such actions also made him appear cautious and professional, savvy, or perhaps even cowardly. The checks taken from the burglarized car were never cashed. My dad's jewelry was never pawned. He didn't take my dad's credit cards to begin with. He left certain valuables onsite. He was not seen leaving. He might have shut off his phone. He hasn't talked. Hasn't re-offended (or he'd be fingerprinted and swabbed for DNA). Hasn't been caught. He ran away when confronted on the street. Why had those confrontations not ended in violence too?

And certain actions made him appear stupid. Appearing on this list, too, are many of the traits on the "brazen" list, like burglarizing cars on a street where people are coming home from work. But trying to break into a safe with garden shears takes the cake. This person was either very stupid—or the crime scene was very staged.

When I considered all of this together, I just couldn't get over certain inconsistencies. If the perpetrator was the car burglar, we would have an individual who ran away from a soccer mom when she confronted him—yet who entered an occupied residence, walked upstairs to the room with activity in it, and iced my father. We have someone so savvy that they never cashed the stolen checks, never pawned the stolen jewelry, and have kept their nose clean ever since—but someone so stupid they thought they could get into a safe with garden shears. It just didn't add up.

Over the course of the intervening years, I learned that many of these assumptions and even some of the "facts" were either incorrect or uncertain.

But for the first year—nay, the first several years—after my father's death, all of us close to the case—my friends, my family, and anyone I discussed the case with—agreed that only one of two scenarios made sense.

(1) The killer was a neighborhood kid who had a drug problem. Perhaps he lived with his grandma, because his parents were out of the picture. On the night in question, he decided to become a "badass" by getting ahold of a gun and breaking into cars. He entered the house but shot my dad by mistake, perhaps because he really did need a fix. In the week after my dad's killing, grandma saw the news coverage. She had noticed little Jimmy coming home that night sweaty, shaken, and wearing the same clothes described in the sketch. Wanting to protect her grandson, she asked no questions, but sent him to rehab and then to live with her stern brother in Mississippi. He has not re-offended and has told no one about that day.

OR

(2) There was more to it.

Words of a Dead Man

By early December, between the family members working on the task, and the police, we finally got access to my father's emails. All of desperately wanted to see if there were any clues therein. Had my father been involved in a business deal that went sour? Was he dating some woman we didn't know about?

My father was rather disorganized in life, and to say his home was cluttered was an understatement. So you can imagine the state of his e-mail inboxes. We started the long process of going through them.

Alas, we found nothing but a father who was pained about family squabbles and was going to do something about it. His words were hard to read. On July 22, 2013, he wrote his dear friend Al Jones, about my sister's boyfriend: *they knew when I was onto the scam and now do not come around any more...problem is, it costs me 3000 each time I have my trust updated...just can't see leaving anything to the pricks my daughter Nicole chooses to share her bed from time to time.*

[Nicole] has a boy friend who claimed to be an architect from Berkeley and who took her over the falls with bullshit...has not been employed for ten years, cost the family 20,000 in a law suit to evict a tenant from Nicole's property.

Nicole neither speaks or communicates with any of her siblings, and now me. It has put me on a mind fuck.

On August 6, 2013, he wrote Jones, "*I have offered to transfer my stocks to the girls and to Michael's kids just in case Nicole goes postal.*"

On September 22, 2013, my father wrote:

I have not spoken to Nicole for some time and confronted her with an offer to [provide her money to settle her legal dispute] . . . It seems so godamn (sic) stupid. . . . The last time I knew Nicole was on Bright lane [i.e., in my dad's house], she asked to borrow a bolt cutter and left off a bracelet to be repaired...not one word was spoken, in fact I had to mail the bracelet back to her and never received word that she got it or a thank you for repairing. The bolt cutter has not been returned either. . . .

Mark is evidently not working...paints a wall once in a while or gets a load of shit for the garden from the zoo...but a contributor to the bread bill, or the cheese spread is not forthcoming...nicole hauls herself off to work, while he sleeps late, [she] put the asshole on her health plan and he will not sell one godamn toy to help her with the bills. Sooner or later she will get upset with the boy toy. . . .

Wednesday, I took Damian to the Rosebowl for his second manual transmission driving lesson and while waiting for Damian... Mark drove up about 10:00 and here we were face to face with small talk. He asked if we could have lunch... sure says I... call me friday... he never did... and there he was with a shit eaten grin... what a prick.

On November 12, 2013, he wrote, "*Nicole and Mark used the handyman who did work for me, but since they no longer speak to me, I know if I asked them for his number, they would tell me to get fucked.*"

It made me sad to think my father had died thinking his family was in disarray.

MORE TIPS

The life of a family member of a murder victim is lonely. Some days, I felt like I was the only one who remembered my dad's case was unsolved, and the only person obsessing over it.

The sense of disillusionment was heightened by the heartbreaking nature of certain "tips." Lots of people who reached out didn't always have his best interest in mind, or all of their wits about them. In late 2015, for example, after some of the "it's been two years" retrospectives came out, a woman left a message on my office voice mail on the weekend. My staff said her message "sounded kooky" but of course I had to call her back and hear what she had to say. Alas my staff was right. She wasn't playing with a full deck.

As the family member in the public eye, I became a sort of clearinghouse for such calls. I didn't mind—I don't know who staffs the LAPD tip line, who followed up, or whether the public felt comfortable calling it. At least in my case, I evaluated each and every tip that came in, and passed all but the craziest to the detectives working directly on my dad's case.

Was it easy? No. When someone calls with "100% valuable information you want to hear about your dad's case"—it gets your hopes up. For a few fleeting moments until you reach that person, you wonder, "what if this is the tip that breaks the case wide open?" And then, as you sit there listening to minute ten of someone—who often just needs to talk to someone themselves—drone on and on about a dream they had, or a homeless guy on their street—your spirit sinks. And you feel time slipping away.

Nothing was more painful than the people who toyed with my emotions to prosecute their own vendettas. Three separate times, someone called me to tell me that the guy in the sketch was right outside their home. One even went so far as to say that the annoying homeless guy had disappeared right after my father's murder, but now was back. So I would race over, the police would eventually arrive, and yet all three times it became manifestly clear that these three different people had not been able to get a transient cleared from in front of their homes, so they tried to use me to do it. It's difficult to express how used I felt at those moments. And how isolating it is to be taken advantage of by people who know you're vulnerable.

GETTING ORGANIZED

With all the emotions, the frenetic pace of life, and the zillions of clues, some trivial or some seemingly significant, I knew I needed to get organized. I started making extensive notes about everything I knew: a sort of table of facts. I had gotten excellent grades in law school not from any particular skill I believe, nor because I was smarter than anyone else—simply because I was well-organized. So I began recording everything I learned that was factual—and then created a table of inferences that tended to stem from those facts. I paid particular attention to timelines and things we knew with certainty. And then I questioned my own facts: I tried to ask, "why does this NOT make sense?"

Once my first draft was done, I asked the detectives if we could meet so I could ask some of the questions that I was asking myself. As luck would have it, one of the pair was headed to Sacramento for a law-enforcement conference, and we sat down together to chat for a bit.

I brought my document, and I could see he was sort of taken aback when I said I couldn't share it with him. Don't get me wrong: I shared with them the contents—all the facts I had written out, I either verbalized to them, or, where appropriate, put in an email. We discussed literally everything, most often on marathon phone calls.

But in those days, I hadn't shared the document with anyone because of my knowledge of the law. I knew two things: (a) any document I share with the police becomes part of the file, a public record; and (b) to convict someone, the standard is "guilty beyond a reasonable doubt."

I had a concern: Let's say someone was finally arrested. They catch the young punk who did it. They are rather certain it is him, but the case, for whatever reason, is not a slam dunk, and the perpetrator hires a defense attorney, bent on making himself famous in this high-profile case. Now my dossier contained every little clue—literally a dozen different theories. It contained my suspicions on every possible suspect—from Donald Trump (kidding!) to unnamed archetypes (a jilted lover). It was, in sum, a document that could create a reasonable doubt. For years I refused to share any part of it, because I shuddered at the thought of some defensive lawyer for the real murderer stating something like, "well here's the written statement of Joseph Gatto's son Mike, who knew him pretty well. And Mike details, right here on page 83, a laundry list of reasons the 'real murderer' could have been Joseph Gatto's old army buddy who had a grudge…"

I learned later my concerns were probably overblown, but that scenario still gives me nightmares. I don't practice criminal law, and I probably knew just enough to get myself all riled up. But still I did not want to share my notes with the detectives, and they seemed very annoyed by this.

TIDBITS AND DETAILS

As I recorded everything that might be relevant, I logged a bunch of minor details from the police, my father's neighbors, and what we could piece together from his electronic devices and e-mails.

He had visited his accountant in July 2013, telling him he was changing his estate plan, and asking him for a referral. He told his first cousin the same thing on the same day. His insurance agent informed us that in August 2013, he had changed the executor of his policy to me. From October 14 through October 22, 2013, he had ordered Change in Beneficiary forms for most of his major accounts, from stocks to CDs. These forms are used to change who gets an account upon death. He left the forms in plain sight at his house. Both my sisters had keys to his house, and I suppose it's possible someone could have copied their sets.

On the day of his murder, according to his across-the-street neighbor, both homeowners whose properties actually touched my father's were coincidentally out of town. At midday on November 12, a sedan (perhaps a Toyota according to the witness), with two males inside, one Hispanic, went zooming up my father's tiny street, very fast. They made a U-turn at the top of the street and drove back down. At 4pm on November 12, the male neighbor across the street, as he had done for about two weeks, left for his night-shift gig, shooting a commercial.

At about 6:50pm on November 12, the female neighbor across the street, left, as she regularly did, to take her son to his guitar lesson. She was "90% certain" that my dad's garage door was closed. At 7pm, the caretaker for the only other neighbor on the street, my father's ~80-year-old friend with dementia, went home for the day, as she did every night.

Four houses were in close proximity to my father—two across the street, and two abutting his, but technically on other streets. And somehow, no one was home that night. How does a murder occur in the middle of a big city like Los Angeles, at a time when there was not a single potential witness at home?

GETTING BY, WITH HELP

The first fifty days after my father's murder were a blur. I don't remember sleeping much, and many days it was hard to function. I was lucky to have a strong support system around me.

I remember an old interview with Frank Sinatra, where a male journalist, seeking advice, asked Sinatra, "What do you do when a woman cries?" Sinatra' replied, "Cry with her." During the first fifty days, Danielle and I cried a lot together. (But unlike Sinatra's paradigm, I think she cried more with me than the other way around.) Both emotionally and in helping with the banal details of life, Danielle was an absolute rock. And I know she had to work hard at it, because even though it wasn't her father who got killed, she was going through many of the same emotions I was. My daughters were also sources of tremendous respite for me, without knowing it. Just seeing their little smiling faces, so young, reminded me of the meaning of life.

During this time, I also funded a scholarship in my dad's name for arts and other "non-traditional" students. I had always felt that there were plenty of resources available for many other categories, but the lower-middle-class unconventional student, who wanted to go to art, design, or trade school, had fewer. I made the initial contributions, but I was so deeply moved at the others who stepped up to contribute to. I thought my father would approve of the act of making even a small difference in the lives of students in need.

My team was also so supportive. I had focused mostly on hiring brilliant and capable young people, mentoring them as best as I could, and letting them flourish. They did not let me down. Don't get me wrong, I had my share of tested veterans, who had seen it all, and who probably guided me more than I guided them. Folks like my my District Director, Jason Insalaco; my Campaign Director, Stacey Brenner, my Chief of Staff, John Ferrera; and my Legislative Director, Aaron Moreno; All of them stepped up and kept everything running smoothly in my physical and psychological absence. My junior staff was absolutely stellar too. Folks like Taylor Giroux, Denni Ritter, Eric Menjivar, Katerina Robinson, and Elena Semerdjian. Looking back, it is no surprise to me that my junior staff have gone on to become absolute superstars.

I can imagine the conversations that they had to have during these times. "Sorry, the Assemblyman can't meet with you that day because he's attending a news conference to ask the public for help in his dad's murder." Or, "sorry, the Assemblyman can't meet with you today because he's just not in a good place right now." They kept the office afloat during tough times.

BACK TO WORK

In 2014, a new legislative year started, and I had to go back to work on behalf of my 500,000 constituents. Those early days of 2014 made for some interesting conversations.

One politician, with a legendary mean streak, who has been in and out of politics for over two decades, openly mocked me. "You were nothing before your dad died. Now that's all you're known for." While I knew this was false—I was chairman of the Appropriations Committee, the fourth most-powerful elected position in the state—and I had done a lot of good in my three years in the legislature. I still use's this guy's remark as motivation to do more. I would tell my staff, "I don't want to be remembered as the guy whose dad was murdered during my time in office. I want to be remembered as the guy who authored important legislation and reformed the things needing reform."

I also told myself I wouldn't let it change me. An old-timer in the Capitol reminded me of a great mantra:

"anecdotes make bad law." Meaning, you can't assume your personal experiences are the experiences of the population as a whole. For example, there was one elderly, farsighted state senator who had trouble reading her prescription instructions. So she tried to mandate the font size and type on pill bottles statewide. Making the switch to her preferred type would have cost a lot of mom-and-pop pharmacies a lot of money—this was in the era of older printers and high healthcare costs.

"Anecdotes make bad law," I reminded myself. I didn't want to start assuming the worst about humanity in my legislating. So I resolved two things: That I was going to share my experiences with my fellow lawmakers, but I would never politicize my father's killing, or let it cloud my logic on criminal-justice issues.

Criminal justice in the U.S. tends to be on a pendulum. We alternate between periods of, "lock 'em all up and throw away the key" and "all criminals are just misunderstood souls who, if given an education, wouldn't rob and kill." The truth lies somewhere in between. I was already fairly moderate—even leaning conservative—on law-and-order issues. I worked hard to maintain that balance so I wouldn't become a jihadist based on my sorrow and desire for justice.

REWARDS AND RAIDS

Early 2014 also brought two additional developments, which we pursued with vigor and hope, but which turned out to be fruitless. First, the LA City Council offered a $50,000 reward for information leading to my father's killer. This is the standard reward in Los Angeles.

As an aside, I get asked occasionally whether I think I received special treatment from authorities in my father's case. My answer is a resounding no—and I relay the example of the reward. Not a single dollar more was offered, despite the high profile and frustrating mysteries of my father's case.

I was considered a good fundraiser in politics as I had a good network of supportive friends. As an upstart given little chance of winning and with little support from political PACs, I had raised about $1.4 million in 2009 for my first run for office. While in office, I had raised much more, and given much away. I also raised a lot of money for charities.

So naturally I asked the police if I could give or raise additional funds to the reward kitty, to make it more enticing. I was initially shocked at their reply—although in retrospect I realize it was right. "No," they said. "We don't want it to look like we are giving you special treatment." While I was initially depressed by this, I realized they were right. We shouldn't send a message that any particular life is worth more than another.

Also around this time, the police raided the homes of parole violators, known burglars, and probationers in the neighborhoods around my father's. Almost 100 such raids occurred. No one was found to have a connection to the case. No one talked about a friend who had been involved, or gossip they may have heard, to collect the reward or get leniency on their sentences.

In other words, both the raids and the rewards, frustratingly, led to nothing.

MORE NOTHING

In February 2014, I had a long and freewheeling discussion with the detectives, with several follow-ups. I thanked them and told them how much I valued these discussions. Besides being a naturally curious person, I was still worried for my family. Besides being a regular, caring family member of a murder victim, I myself fielded questions everywhere I went. I had seen the Mayor and Police Chief recently, and they had asked me how the case was going. To this, the detectives kind of chuckled, "we purposefully don't tell the Chief and Mayor everything." I wondered what this meant, but just decided to let it go.

They told me they had run the fingerprints through every available database nationwide, including government applicants. To me, that was yet another indicator that the crime was very simple—or very complicated. The perpetrator had either been someone young without much of a record—or an imported hitman. Although I acknowledge too, that much of this hinged on some of the unknown prints being those of the killer. The prints could, in theory, be those of some elderly person garage-sale holder—or they could be so incomplete to be unusable.

The detectives also claimed they did a "massive tower dump" in the area and were going through phone numbers. It is my understanding this is imperfect too, and can produce a lot of false positives and negatives. Moreover, my father lived one house away from a 2.5-mile artificial lake, which thousands of people used as a walking track each day. But in general, this also militated in favor of a very simple crime, or a very complicated one. The killer either didn't use his phone, or perhaps didn't own one, or was savvy enough to shut it off completely that day.

The killer had left the bullet cartridge behind. This too, indicated it was someone really sloppy or someone who did not care. It was either a total amateur, or someone who was confident that he or she would never be caught.

They reiterated their thought that my dad might have reached for his phone or something else (something I can't imagine him doing), and that the shot might have been accidental.

But the most interesting fact they disclosed was this: despite the car burglar being confronted by two different adults, including one adult male, the only person who saw the alleged gun was the then eight-year-old boy. The adult's 911 call had not mentioned it. If you take away the gun, this seemingly significant car burglary becomes a random property crime, likely unrelated.

CHANGED BEHAVIOR

After the immediate tasks pertaining to my father's death and funeral were done, after the melancholy of the holidays that year was over, and after I settled back into a somewhat normal daily routine, I noticed some pretty serious behavioral changes in myself. I counted six, but there were probably more.

The first one was I kept a newspaper reporting my dad's murder on my nightstand at all times. Why? Well, I kept waking up in the middle of the night thinking it had been a dream. I've heard people talk about this before, and I always assumed it was something out of the movies. But the cliché, "I felt like it was all a bad dream" really does describe how I felt. For the first six months or so after my father's death, I would wake up at night with a profound sense of disbelief that it had happened. Thus, the newspaper.

The second change I noticed was an obsession with watching garage doors close. The police had told me that my father's killer likely slipped into or rolled under his slowly closing garage door as he retrieved something from his car, or as he returned home, or when he had left. The lack of any signs of forced entry never sat well with me, and the idea that humans could be so vulnerable to a slowly closing garage door worried me. If you're like most people, you probably close the garage door as you enter the main part of your house, absentmindedly, often with full hands, and go about your day. Not me. Despite what is probably an infinitesimally small number of burglars entering homes by ducking unnoticed under slowly closing garage doors, I started to make sure obsessively that our garage door had closed. I mean I sat and watched it close, every inch. I still do this, to this day.

The third change involved television. You don't realize until you live through a violent act how obsessed American television is with violent acts. Until you picture a loved one dying by a handgun blast, you don't realize how often such acts are portrayed in excruciating detail on television. In fact, it's hard to avoid such depictions any given night. Don't get me wrong, I never watched much TV anyway, but after my dad's murder, I couldn't watch much at all. Shows like *How To Get Away With Murder* made me sick. I didn't want to see anyone's father blown away, even fictionally. For a few years, I just couldn't handle seeing that type of violence on screen. I can report to you that at time of writing, I've been *re-desensitized* to violent depictions on screen, like every other American.

The fourth change was what I would call changed memories, or more accurately, "ruined memories." When I was growing up in Silver Lake, the community stairs were the source of so many positive memories for me and my friends, because we often hung out there. They were semi-private, shaded areas, with built-in seats of sorts, and great views. On those stairs is where we sneaked our first beer and had many of our first kisses with neighborhood girls. It's where we had profound discussions about life, and made hopeful pronouncements about the future. Before my dad's murder, I always felt a twinge of positive nostalgia when I drove by the community stairs. Now I don't. I see a path leading to darkness, because of the simple assertion that my father's killer may have traversed them on the way to do the deed.

The fifth change could more accurately be described as a phobia, and today I still struggle to explain it fully. Because of my position in the Legislature, I took between two to six flights a week. And after my father's death, I went from a "nothing phases me; flying is fun" person, to someone with a phobia of flying. I'm not sure why. I did notice that the phobia was only there when I flew alone. If my family was with me, it wasn't present. I believe therefore that losing my father had made me part consciously, part subconsciously, consider what my young family would do without me. And that thought is what caused the phobia.

The sixth change involved how I lived my life. If I had to put it kindly, I would say I lived life more in the moment. If I had to put it pejoratively, I'd say I lived a little more recklessly. If I had to describe it evenhandedly, I'd say that I made a conscious effort to live life with a little more gusto, but that I didn't always make the right decisions. I took more road trips than usual. I had never been materialistic, but I focused even more on experiences than before. But I also drank more than I should've. I believe this phase took almost three years to pass. But I understand that such behavior is common.

Looking back, I was probably aware of the first four of these as they happened, but the fifth only with hindsight and reflection.

I INTERVIEW THE WITNESSES, PART I

By September 2014, I had so many questions about our lead suspect, that I thought I should personally interview the woman who, coming home from karate, had seen the car burglar. I also wanted to speak with the man, her neighbor, who had given chase initially on foot, and then with her in her car. So I asked around the neighborhood, got their phone numbers, and simply called them.

The woman was helpful, although still traumatized. It had not been easy stepping forward. She had fielded zillions of calls from everyone from CNN to the local news, because in the days after my father's killing, everyone had wanted an interview.

She told me many interesting things. First, she said that the car burglar looked like, "an Eastern European hitman." That he was casual, lithe, and unrushed. That he did not seem high on drugs.

However, there were some inconsistencies between what I had heard before, and even between the couple times we spoke. For example, she was not sure whether he had said, "do you want to die tonight?" or "take another step and it's the end." Although he dressed like he was foreign, she was pretty sure he had not spoken with an accent. She also gave two slightly different time windows when we spoke on two separate occasions.

Critically, she had never seen his face and never seen a gun. Within her family, only her son had seen both.

When they tried to pursue him in her car (by driving around the loop he had taken a shortcut to, by taking the stairs), a truck blocked their path for quite some time. She said she thought it was a decoy.

I INTERVIEW THE WITNESSES, PART II

Next I spoke with the neighbor she had fetched, whose assistant owned the car he was breaking into. He confirmed that the car burglar did not seem rushed or high, and that there was no shouting. He said the car burglar "looked Armenian, not Hispanic."

I also learned that a woman had seen the person of interest clearly, as she was coming up the stairs as he fled down them. Despite our public pleas, she had not stepped forward.

The male neighbor also revealed that he and the boy had come up with entirely different sketches, causing the sketch artist to give up momentarily. He had told the police that he simply had not gotten a good enough view to even provide a sketch in the first place. Yet only his, as the adult's, was the one circulated to the public.

I wondered why the police had allowed this to happen, as the sketch could have been way off. I worried that someone might have seen a sweaty and nervous neighborhood troublemaker return home that evening, but said, "I'm probably being too harsh—he just doesn't look anything like the sketch Assemblyman Gatto circulated." I felt like a fool.

MILESTONES AND
A NEW TRADITION

2014 went by with many milestones, many of them breathlessly noted in the media. In December, just a couple months after my father's slaying, the newspapers ran stories like, "Gatto family marks the holidays without their patriarch." In June, they ran stories like, "Mike Gatto celebrates his first Father's Day without his dad." Then of course, in November 2014, there were the stories like, "We can't believe it's been a year since the Gatto slaying." In November 2014, we held a press conference with the police to beg the public to come forward with information that would help solve the case. No one did.

At the time, I was naïve. I couldn't believe a year had passed with no break. I think everyone who goes through having a family member murdered believes the crime will be solved in weeks. Law enforcement event has a term for this: CSI Effect, after the noted TV series where every loose end gets tied up with precision after about an hour. And many murders *are* solved in a few weeks. I would often read about a murder that first appeared to be a mystery, but then, always less than a month later, the police got some key surveillance footage, or someone stepped forward with a clue, or someone figured out that it was a business dispute gone awry, etc. With my dad's case, none of that had happened.

Also around that time, I made a resolution that I wasn't going to let the grief kill me. I told you how I felt like I really never got to know my father. 17 years in his house, and he had worked most of them. And I was a typical disengaged teenager during many of them. Then, college, law school, and a busy life. This magnified the grief that one feels with losing a loved one to a murder.

But I had a conversation with my friend Baruch midway toward November, and he had said quietly, "you know in my faith, we grieve for 11 months after the death of a parent. The ancient tradition of putting a timeline to it, in many ways, helps you move beyond it." That conversation sparked an epiphany in me. I was obsessed with helping find his killer. And with getting his civil affairs to be resolved orderly. Yet neither of those showed any signs of resolving soon. I realized: if I added years of grief to that, it would probably kill me. So, I quietly resolved to borrow this ancient wisdom from Judaism, and try to adhere to the traditional period of mourning.

We also had to make a conscious effort to make sure our kids had a normal life around November.

November is a wonderful month in Sacramento. The air gets cold; the leaves start changing color on some trees, and of course, there is Thanksgiving, my favorite holiday. Danielle and I didn't want our children's Novembers to be dominated by somber memorials of their grandfather's death—hearing me do interview after interview, and watching me mope around the house. So Danielle came up with the idea, after the vigils had passed and after the interviews had subsided, and after they visited their grandfather's grave, to take a day off and take them to Disneyland. It sounds corny, but we didn't want their Novembers to be all sadness, and around November 12, I was pretty much useless, so we turned to the "Happiest Place on Earth."

FAMILIAL DNA

In one of my conversations with the police after about a year had gone by, they mentioned that beyond uploading the standard DNA loci to the FBI's database, they could also check Familial DNA. Familial DNA is a little different. It's a California program, which uses patterns on the Y-Chromosome, inherited by males only, to compare to other serious offenders in the database. It has been used to solve some stubborn cold cases over the years. This program, state-run, and specific to male relatives, should not be confused with the federal crime database (CODIS), or with solving crimes using general genealogical DNA websites to solve crimes, like Ancestry.com and 23AndMe.

There were certain criteria for using the Familial DNA program—the case had to be pretty much cold, and the police had to have pretty much exhausted all leads. As you can see, these criteria are subjective and a bit amorphous. The police asked whether I would call California Attorney General Kamala Harris to ask if my dad's case could qualify. I did. She was once again, immensely sympathetic and kind. After reviewing where things stood in the case, she said that we did qualify for the program.

I was optimistic this would bear fruit. The tragic reality is that many males who lead a life of crime, come from families where other males have committed serious crimes too. A father who served time for bank robbery often has a son who gets in trouble too. A brother who commits a drive-by shooting might have male cousins in the same gang. So, the police accessed the program, and we waited for results.

It's now been several years, and despite this wider range of possibilities, we still haven't gotten a hit. Frustratingly, this indicates one of three things: (1) the perpetrator comes from a family that has mostly been law-abiding. This supports the "neighborhood kid, high on drugs" theory. Or (2) this was something totally crazy, like an imported hitman, who of course would not have family in the California databases. Or (3) most alarmingly, the DNA on the tools was simply from someone who touched them at a garage sale.

THE JOSEPH GATTO HIGHWAY

The end of 2014 also brought something truly special. On one of the last days of the legislative session in August, my staff had shuffled me off the floor briefly, and told me to prepare for something special. Next, Assemblymember (now Congressman) Jimmy Gomez and Majority Leader Ian Calderon rose to present a resolution to name the stretch of highway by the arts school my had founded after my father.

And it wasn't just any arts school. My father's students, many of whom hadn't done as well in "traditional" schools, had absolutely flourished in an art-focused school, just as he predicted. Among his former students were Kehinde Wiley, the brilliant sculptor and painter who painted President Obama's formal portrait; actress Jenna Elfman; singer Josh Groban; and director Jane Wu (of Blue Eye Samurai), among many others.

So naming the freeway near the school after my father was deeply touching, and I was profoundly moved. In large part because few people had ever successfully surprised me in my life, but my colleagues had managed to do so, in a place that is not conducive to keeping secrets. But most of all, because it was something very nice to do for a nice man. Highways are often named after astronauts and politicians. But here was the state of California naming a highway for a teacher. Someone who had dedicated his life—even when past the point of retiring for 100% of his salary—to teaching the next generations. It is important for society to honor people like that, who spend their lives quietly fulfilling a sense of duty, sharing their passions so they can take root in others.

On November 14, 2014, the new freeway signs were unveiled, and they were installed shortly thereafter. I still get a kick out of seeing them when I drive on the Interstate 10 just east of downtown. I still get phone calls from people whose lives my father affected, who get excited when they see the signs for the first time. And my kids happily call out from the backseat, "that's Gramps' sign!"

A FULL-TIME JOB

In all of 2014, and really from the end of 2013 through the end of 2016, my father's case was a full-time job for me. I thought about it every day; perhaps obsessed over it, is a more apt description. It took up a lot of space in my head and my soul. I tried to help get his estate organized. He had not expected to die of course, so his affairs were not in order. There were so many legal issues to address. I had to deal with the items I inherited. I'm an ascetic minimalist; my father was an aggregative maximalist. Imagine getting dumped on you an unorganized milk crate filled with old dusty items. Some pieces are valuable antiques; some pieces' only value was as kindling. This summarized much of my father's collections. Except instead of a milk crate, it was a moving truck or two!

And most importantly, I tried to guide the police; I tried to get questions answered; and I tried to ensure that they don't forget about the case. All of this together took around forty hours a week. I had to balance this with my duties to advance legislation in the capitol; to analyze and vote on the legislation of others; to take care of my constituents' needs in my district; and most importantly, to be a good husband and father. Let's just say I didn't sleep much. Because as much as I devoted time to my father's case, I devoted more to my family. They were my only respite from what seemed to me to be a wicked world.

Looking back: while I certainly don't miss the frenetic pace—not at all—I do feel sad about how the case has progressed—indeed, how all cold cases progress. In late 2013, I spoke with the LAPD every day. Then, at some point, it became once a week. Then, once a month. After a few years: once a quarter. Now I probably talk with them once a year. This is the nature of a cold case. The conversations get repetitive. The detectives get impatient with the questions. "If there is any news, you'll be the first to know." Or an impatient, "yes, we've considered that theory." I am certain that I became an absolute pest for the detectives in my case, and when I went above them—to other personnel in the department, to the chief, or to the Mayor I'm sure—they hated me for it. But what was I supposed to do? I often ran into Mayor Garcetti at events. "How's your dad's case?" he would ask. Occasionally I vented, and I know that led to my frustrations being taken out on the detectives. Sometimes they deserved it. But I could not imagine being less engaged. After all, I owe it to my father and to justice to explore every lead and to keep the people investigating the case motivated.

AN INTERESTING THEORY

It's no secret to anyone in online marketing, and probably not to most people anymore. Businesses that send an email can see if you read it, see what you clicked, and how many times you did either. They do this by embedding a tiny pixel in the emails they send (a tiny image) that auto-loads, pinging their servers every time the email is opened. They can use a similar method for tracking who clicked on links.

My father's case generated a lot of media stories, which many media outlets would e-mail to their large distribution lists, as there was a lot of interest in his case. The media interest stayed pretty steady, especially on the milestones or anniversary dates.

One such outlet contacted me after running a story featuring a link to the LAPD sketch. One user, a woman (they knew her name) had clicked on the sketch something like 450 times. Is it possible, the publisher asked, that this woman knew the person of interest, or thought she knew him, and was obsessively clicking on the sketch, in disbelief or horror? Assuming this woman didn't step forward, could the police perhaps coax some help out of her if they contacted her affirmatively?

I liked this creative thinking, and I so appreciated receiving this tip. I did what I did with all interesting or remotely credible tips: passed it on to the investigators. I don't believe anything came of it; I don't even know for sure that they contacted her.

I later learned that e-mail marketing can generate false positives. For example, if someone leaves an organization, and the organization generates an auto-reply, "John Smith is no longer with Acme Corp…", that can register as four or more "opens" or "clicks." I also learned that some peoples' inbox settings can make a preview panel look like an "open," which would mean that this user might have actually read or replied to an email above the media outlet's, many times, and the "preview" of the media email was what was registering. This person could have also forwarded the email to a hundred people in the area, or a listserv, hoping to help catch the criminal. In such cases, the people to whom the e-mail was forwarded count as being read by the original sender. In other words, there could be logical explanations for the shocking number of opens or clicks, and we haven't even discussed yet a computer error or some odd loop in an email inbox.

Still, the number seemed excessive and possible relevant. And I hoped it led to a great tip, but like all others so far, my hopes were dashed.

MEANWHILE IN THE CAPITOL

In late 2014, I was contacted by other people who had had a family member murdered, as well as some members of law enforcement, to alert me to a troubling development. A California Court of Appeal (an intermediate appellate court) had struck down California's 11-year-old DNA-collection law, which required samples be taken from people arrested for a serious felony. If that decision stood, cases like my dad's—and thousands of other murders and rapes— would likely remain unsolved.

One of the profound blessings about being in office, especially in a state that moves as fast legislatively as California, is the ability to right wrongs by changing the law. Also, the Legislature has the ability to abrogate (or reject) court decisions in the state that are not based purely on constitutional grounds. So in January 2015, I jumped into action. After carefully reading the Court of Appeals' issues with California's DNA-collection practices, I wrote legislation that would go into effect if the Supreme Court upheld the appellate decision.

I'm generally low key. I didn't advertise that this bill could affect my father's case—particularly because at that time, I didn't share <u>any</u> of the details (like the fact we had DNA evidence) with anyone, out of respect for the police's wishes. (At that time, the police still had not shared many details publicly.) As the year went on, I shepherded this bill through committee after committee and got it to its final stop before reaching the entire house for a vote.

I had been tangentially involved in a battle for the speakership in late 2013. I had been contacted by many asking me to run, and after declining, I had initially (and quietly) backed a friend of mine who was interested. But mostly I hadn't done anything for anyone, because the bulk of the speakership battle occurred in the late Fall of 2013, when, to put it mildly, I was distracted. In politics however, being late to the dance is almost the same as not attending. I don't think the person who eventually won the speakership felt too warm and fuzzy about me, and she thought I had come over to her side too late. When she took over, she stripped me of my chairmanship of the powerful Appropriations Committee, in favor of one of her main lieutenants. Although I didn't find this fair (I considered her a friend, and a thoughtful lawmaker, and ended up supporting her wholeheartedly as much as I could given what I was going through), I knew it was part of politics.

What happened to my bill though, was unfortunate. The way the Appropriations Committee works in California is different from the federal congress, where the committee appropriates funds that have been loosely set by the budget. Instead, in California, the committee "scores" each non-budgetary bill, by assigning a cost to the proposal. For example, if you wrote legislation to require the department of motor vehicles to offer hand sanitizer to anyone taking a driver's test, the committee would tally the number of driving tests and the number of DMV offices and the average use of hand sanitizer, and the average cost per gallon, and then assess how much such a bill—which is non-budgetary—would cost the state. Then, the committee chair, together with the Speaker, engage in a cost-benefit analysis to determine whether the bill lives or dies. There is no vote, in the conventional sense. This is why the committee is so powerful.

The Committee has a reputation for being very political too. Members are asked to rank their bills still alive by the time they reach the Appropriations Committee, and the Speaker makes an effort to make sure all members of the majority party are taken care of. Most members get their #1 priority bill out of the Appropriations Committee so it can advance to a floor vote.

With no public statements that we had DNA in my dad's case, and no grandstanding on my part, the bill probably came across to many as a wonky, very technical and legalistic bill that addressed some arcane criminal-justice decision. But, because of the profound need for this bill, I ranked it as my #1 that year.

When the hearing occurred at the end of May, I felt like I was punched in the gut. The chairman announced into the microphone that the bill was, "held in committee." Many Capitol insiders thought the message was clear, "You didn't get on the team early enough. So we're going to guillotine your number- one priority." I also genuinely believe that the average member of the legislature (and the leadership) certainly wasn't tracking this issue as closely as I did.

Victims' groups were furious. Crime Victims United and I issued a joint statement.

Last December, the California Court of Appeal quietly struck down all of California's DNA-testing laws, which are used to solve the most serious crimes. An appeal is pending before the California Supreme Court. If the high court does not overturn the intermediate court's decision (and that outcome is in doubt), hundreds of thousands of California families awaiting justice for a murdered loved one, and hundreds of thousands of rape victims, will see their chances of obtaining justice greatly diminished.

The legislative process is old-fashioned, technical, and slow, and the Legislature remains a place that rarely speaks with uniformity on any issue. It is therefore highly doubtful that the Legislature could react to a bad Supreme Court decision with the necessary rapidity to ensure that millions of criminals do not go free without being tested to solve other crimes.

Assembly Bill 84 was a rare example of the Legislature planning ahead to anticipate a less-than-ideal outcome, and had passed with bipartisan support and the support of crime-victims groups.

Today, the Assembly Appropriations Committee and Assembly leadership took a huge gamble on the outcome of a lengthy and complicated case by holding AB 84, in effect killing it for this legislative session. Sadly, they chose political gamesmanship over victims' families. Words cannot express our disappointment at this outcome, and we will do everything it takes to ensure that there is no lag in DNA testing of our most heinous criminals.

I was genuinely emotional at the outcome. Families like mine "wait by the phone." As irrational as it is, you believe that each week, you may get the call that somebody got picked up for some other felony, got their DNA sampled, and matched the DNA found at the crime scene. You also believe (as I did and still do) that if there is a lag in testing, thousands of criminals will get arrested without having their DNA swabbed. The thought that my father's killer could be among them was deeply troubling.

I told the media, "One of the hardest speeches I've ever had to give was to explain to my children why their grandfather was not coming home again... For a lot of families like mine, you're waiting for that phone call from law enforcement that forensic evidence has led to a lead in that case."

I then lashed out on Twitter—which I had never done before at my fellow Democrats in the legislature. I expressed hurt and frustration, and I revealed that the bill had personal ramifications for my father's case.

Lo and behold, a couple weeks later, the Speaker agreed to allow my proposal to move forward; indeed, to come onto the legislation as a co-author.

Even though I was unhappy at the gamesmanship generally, and I deep-down wished for a legislative process that was less political and more substantive (what would have happened if a crime victim was *not* serving in the Legislature to defend the bill?)—I was pleased that the leadership decided to do the right thing once they learned the significance of the bill.

I told the LA Times: I was "pleased that this misunderstanding is behind us."

APPROACHED TO BE
AN ANTI-GUN SPOKESMAN

Right after my father's funeral, I got asked to attend an event with then-President Barack Obama, where I would say a few words about gun control. I declined. Partly because I was simply exhausted, partly because I didn't want to politicize my dead father, and partly because I had no great answers to express.

Around the time I took a stand for victims' groups and the preservation of DNA testing, I started to get approached regularly by gun-control groups, wanting—or rather expecting—me to become their champion and poster child.

One veteran politico went even further. He saw political gold in my circumstances. He laid out a multi-year plan for me: become an anti-gun crusader, start a foundation, raise lots of money, and use the above as a springboard for higher office.

Everyone assumed that I would start grandstanding on gun issues.

I found it distasteful to use my father's murder for political purposes. For years, I didn't even talk about it unless asked. Not in speeches; not when I presented legislation. This was how the DNA bill had slipped beneath the radar, without my colleagues realizing it was personal for me. Indeed, the only time I spoke about my father's case was when we needed the media to publicize a reward or something—a symbiotic relationship.

But my hesitation to become an anti-gun crusader was deeper than the distaste I felt at politicizing a tragedy. It was because of the magnitude and nuance of the gun issue. I had previously approached the issue with an appreciation for its complexity. Naturally after my father's death, I considered whether I could use my power to prevent other families from going through what we were.

I quickly became disillusioned. No one had any real solutions. I define demagoguery as whenever a politician makes a promise to the most gullible of the people, knowing full well it is impossible. On the gun issue, I found nothing but demagoguery from both sides.

WHY I REJECT DEMAGOGUERY ON GUNS

Much of the political discussions center around "assault weapons" bans. According to the Pew Research Center, in the average year, 14 times more people die from handguns than "assault rifles." So even if you could define an "assault" rifle (and it's hard to avoid just trying to ban guns that look "scary"), you'd probably not prevent long guns from being involved in some murders, and you'd still have 93% of the murders by gun being by handgun—the most basic weapon.

To ban handguns—a pretty core method for people protecting themselves—you'd have to overturn the Second Amendment.

There is so much mythology about the Second Amendment. I regularly have to put on the hat that earned me the top grades at my law school in Constitutional Law, and dispel pop-law misperceptions.

You'd be surprised how many people assert that the Second Amendment should be read to protect only the muskets and rudimentary rifles extant at the time the Constitution was drafted. This logic is problematic. Applied to the First Amendment, we'd only protect print newspapers as free speech, but not television broadcasts, web-based journalism, and social-media posts. This is not how the Constitution works.

You'll often also hear people focus on the phrase, "well-regulated" in the Second Amendment. But the term "regulated" did not mean in 1791 what it means now. There was nothing approaching our modern concept of regulations being the same as laws. "Well-regulated" simply did not have the same meaning. It meant, "well-equipped" and "with proper authority", much like the phrase, "well-appointed" means "having a high standard of equipment" and has nothing to do with appointments or the similar. Those two myths are easy to dispose of.

Slightly more complex is the notion that the Second Amendment only protects gun ownership if one is a member of the militia, a sort of back-up force of volunteer military that can be called up by a state during times of need, or the federal government during times of war.

The drafters of the Second Amendment could have been clearer. Their inclusion of the militia in the Second Amendment kicked off a debate that has lasted centuries. After an exhaustive study of its history, I do believe a primary reason for the Second Amendment was because of many Founding Fathers' fear that a large standing army would allow tyranny like that of European monarchs, one from whom they had just declared independence. Still others wanted to reassure states that they would be allowed to keep independent forces to put down Indian raids and tax rebellions (both common at the time), and to act as a police force when needed—keeping in mind most places had no such thing.

However, words and logic also matter. The founders of the Second Amendment used the term, the "people's rights to keep and bear arms shall not be infringed." It would have been so easy to just say the "militia's right to keep and bear arms." But they didn't.

Moreover, the Second Amendment sits among a long list of 19 individual rights. Things like Free Speech, Freedom of Religion, the right to be secure from unlawful searches, the right to be compensated if the government takes your property, the right to be tried by jury, the freedom from torture, etc. Each one of those inure to individuals, and there is not a single institutional or governmental "right" among them. Indeed, the Bill of Rights was submitted to the states with twelve amendments, not ten. The debate records show that the states explicitly rejected—did not ratify— the ones that changed institutional functions—as they thought it was too premature to do anything that affected the same, choosing to focus on rights instead. So it's hard to argue amidst this sea of individual rights, and having rejected any amendments that dealt with institutions, the Second Amendment was perceived by those who ratified it as covering a right for "the militia" only.

Additionally, the Founding Fathers were concerned about tax rebellions, slave revolts, Indian raids, and invasions from everyone from Spain to the south the Canada from the north. I don't see how a well-functioning militia would work without real people having guns at the ready, on their persons, or at their homes. Indeed there are early laws from colonial days *requiring* men to carry guns into church, to be ready at all times! (It wasn't just the "Minutemen" who were supposed to be ready to fight on a moment's notice."

And finally, even if the Second Amendment was interpreted to apply to the militia only, one can imagine a world where red states declare that all adults who are eligible to buy a gun are part of the militia, much like in colonial times when most people who enjoyed full citizenship rights would be considered part of the militia if they wished. And if the Second Amendment was interpreted to apply to the militia only, the question in blue states would be whether if the state banned or heavily infringed membership to the militia, whether *that* action would be a constitutional violation.

Whatever the case, and independent of my views, the Supreme Court has ruled that the Second Amendment protects individual gun ownership. So, if you wanted to really make a difference on gun proliferation, you'd have to repeal the Second Amendment. Among my Democratic colleagues, I see next to no awareness of this, and even less honesty with the public that this might be their eventual aim.

THE MAGNITUDE OF
THE GUN PROBLEM

So let's repeat: 93% of gun murders—my father's among them—are done with handguns. Handguns are a very basic form of self-protection, covered by the Second Amendment. So, if you want to rid society of large numbers of handguns, you'll have to find a way to infringe on widespread ownership somehow. And that means you'll have to repeal the Second Amendment.

Now I'll indulge the fantasists among you, who may be thinking that this could happen. OK, you say, society changes rapidly. In the span of one generation, our country banned alcohol in the Constitution and then repealed the ban. It could happen with the Second Amendment.

Nevermind for a moment that many scholars believe the Second Amendment just codified an inherent natural right to self protection, which, like the right to parent your own children, was so basic as to not be doubted. Let's imagine the country rose up and banned new gun purchase.

Let me splash some cold water on that. The estimated number of guns already in private ownership in the United States is 434 million. You read that right. Enough for each of the 332 million men, women, and children in the U.S. to each get a gun—and then with 100 million to spare! If you chip away at certain new gun sales—nibble away at the edges, you won't do much at all. And if you banned all new gun sales moving forward, there would still be more than enough in circulation to do all sorts of mischief. Hopefully, you're sensing the magnitude of the problem.

OK, the stalwarts say: once we repeal the Second Amendment and ban all gun sales in the U.S., we'll prohibit private ownership and barter too. Not so fast. Now you'll butt up against another Amendment, the Fifth. You can't take property in the U.S., or render it valueless, without compensating the owners. So, the U.S. would have to buy 434 million guns. At say $250 each, that would cost about $108 billion.

This assumes regular people who just want to defend their inner-city flat from a burglary or their ranch from predation would give up their guns without a fight. It also assumes that criminals—the very people we don't want to have guns—would voluntarily declare how many guns they own and turn them in for purchase. They wouldn't.

So you see how complicated the issue is. And we haven't even started to discuss mental health, the overmedication of young males (with drugs legal and illegal), our violent culture, and the breakdown of a sense of community. All these things affect gun crime.

What sorts of *gun* laws do I favor? Stronger background checks for sure, knowing full well that many of the mass shooters seem like quiet law-abiding people. Mental-health tests, if possible. Making it easier for law enforcement to collect guns from people who are truly deranged. And perhaps a few other minor proposals here and there.

However, the sad truth is that from what I know, none of these would have saved my father.

And very little of the above concepts are discussed with candor or depth as the debates over gun control rage. That bothers me. And it bothers many families of victims. With 93% of gun murders being committed with handguns—and most of these being done by criminals (*i.e.*, not crimes of passion, not mentally ill people, etc.) I've concluded the best way to help families avoid going through what mine did is to find a way to keep cheap handguns from getting in the wrong hands, and to keep people who belong behind bars from getting out prematurely.

If you feel differently than I do, I ask you to forgive my fatalism. It comes from a lifetime of analysis of the issue, and my deeply personal experiences. The bottom line is that the gun issue is not an easy one, and anyone who tries to tell you otherwise—or who spouts platitudes and slogans—should be deeply distrusted.

AN HONOR FROM THE CITY

In June 2015, the city of Los Angeles named an intersection as Joseph Gatto square. It was a few blocks from his house, right across from Ivanhoe elementary, where I had attended kindergarten. It was a really nice gesture from the Mayor and City Council, as I believe they too recognized my father's significance to many former students and community members. The only thing that weighed on me regarding this joyful day was that I missed my flight and didn't make it to the ceremony. My good friend Matthew Sharp stood in for me, and read some prepared words. The city sent me replicas of the metal "Joseph Gatto Square" signs, which I put on my office wall.

Later, both my daughters would attend the same school. I prayed that when they walked by the sign for their grandfather each day, that they'd remember why the city named the square for him, and not the fact that he was taken from them violently.

TWO YEAR-ANNIVERSARY

November 2015 marked two years since the murder, and the community was increasingly bewildered because the crime was still unsolved. So we held a vigil in his neighborhood to keep my father's memory alive, to give people another channel for their grief, and to remind the public that we needed their help to catch my dad's killer.

We marched slowly through my old neighborhood, holding candles in the crisp November cold, singing one of my father's favorite Catholic songs:

I, the Lord of sea and sky, I have heard my people cry.
All who dwell in dark and sin
My hand will save.

I who made the stars of night, I will make their darkness bright.

Who will bear my light to them?
Whom shall I send?
Here I am, Lord.
Is it I, Lord?

I have heard you calling in the night.

I will go, Lord, if you lead me.

I will hold your people in my heart.

I, the Lord of snow and rain, I have borne my people's pain.

I have wept for love of them.

They turn away.

I will break their hearts of stone, give them hearts for love alone.

I will speak my word to them.

Whom shall I send?

Here I am, Lord.

Is it I, Lord?

I have heard you calling in the night.

I will go, Lord, if you lead me.

I will hold your people in my heart.

I can still picture the somewhat confused crowd, winding its way around the path around Silver Lake, quietly singing that song, while many fought back tears. I was one of them.

MORE CLUES

In the Fall of 2015, I had several regularly scheduled brainstorming sessions and update calls with one of the main detectives who was working my father's case. These calls were generally freewheeling and informative.

He told me that my father owned some guns—two ancient rifles, which he had likely bought at garage sales, and one handgun, which they found inside one of my father's safes. I believed this gun had belonged to my grandfather.

I learned that the witnesses had mentioned that the car burglar had passed an Asian woman as he ran down the staircase, and she certainly saw his face, but she had never come forward.

I learned they believed the gun was accidentally discharged. "If he was aiming for your dad's heart [from that close], he wouldn't have missed."

I also learned that there were many sets of unknown prints at my father's house—lots and lots. He told me they were going to subject these prints, many of them partials, to advanced reconstruction and augmentation techniques. But they did say, "this means the perpetrator has never applied for a government job, never been arrested, never left prints at another crime scene, was never caught for being undocumented, and hasn't died inside the country [because apparently they fingerprint unknown corpses]." I was dejected. Again, I thought, "this was either a true crime virgin, or something way more extensive." I pressed the detectives. Was this normal? Is it possible that someone could be so stupid and so violent and so awful, but then never get caught doing anything bad again? "Don't look too much into it," one detective replied. He had a case a few years back where the perpetrator had been arrested eight or nine times but each time, the lazy booking officer had failed to take the fingerprints properly. I remember thinking: this is supposed to be reassuring?

YEARBOOKS

Recall that in my many discussions with the police, we had many times described the profile they had developed of my father's killer—assuming the killer was the one who was the car burglar.

So, a few of our conversations went something like this:

Me: "So, tell me again your thoughts on this kid."

Them: "Well, he was young and the witness claimed he was relatively nicely dressed. He knew exactly where the Community Stairs/Walk Street was, and backed toward it confidently. It's possible the shot was accidental, because he amateurishly freaked out."

Me: "What does that tell you, as to his profile?"

Them: "That he was probably a neighborhood kid."

Me: "That's your theory?"

Them: "Yes."

I didn't doubt the logic. To an outsider, the community stairs that connect the streets in Silver Lake look like they lead to a private home. And yes, while this could just mean the perpetrator had worked out on the stairs before, I recognized it also meant he was likely familiar with my father's neighborhood—assuming again, that the car burglar was the murderer.

So, the next phase in our conversations would always go something like this:

Me: "That part of Silver Lake has—what—a few hundred houses?"

Them: "Yeah. Why?"

Me: "Have you pulled the records from the key census tract, and looked for someone who fits the profile? How many twenty-something kids are living in that neighborhood of two-million-dollar homes?"

You must understand that the hilly parts of Silver Lake—"the Moreno Highlands" or "Prime Silver Lake"—were mostly populated by wealthy gay couples, elderly artists like my father, and the families with very young children that were slowly displacing both. Recall too that we thought the prime candidate was some 23-year-old kid who lived with his grandma, who promptly shipped him off to live with her cousins in Alaska after the killing. How many households fitting that profile could there possibly be nearby?

This was the type of old-fashioned sleuthing that big-city police departments did before the advent of DNA, which has been both a tool and a limitation. This same type of sleuthing—pulling on a thread and seeing if it leads anywhere—is still practiced by some small departments. Nevertheless, despite this being the police's own theory, they did not do this.

Let's give them the benefit of the doubt. Let's assume reviewing census data was not a worthy enough connection to pursue. What about if we had another connection to the car burglar? What if we had visual confirmation?

I further had this conversation about five times with the police.

Me: "OK, so you say you think the perp knew Silver Lake well?"

Them: "Yes."

Me: "You think he may have been a kid from the neighborhood, or one who grew up there?

Them: "Yeah."

Me: "And we have a pretty good guesstimate on his age, based on the eyewitness reports?"

Them: "Yes."

Me: "Silver Lake has only one high school. Have you pulled the yearbooks corresponding with the perp's estimated age range and checked to see who resembles the sketch?"

Again this suggestion was met with pushback. They just didn't have the time, they said, to do things with this depth. They didn't think it would be fruitful. They were busy with other cases. Et cetera.

I wished they would have simply tasked an intern, volunteer, or retiree with this task. Lord knows having the imprimatur of the LAPD plus the latest in facial-recognition technology, plus the ability to go directly to the eyewitnesses, would be the best way to deal with this.

But at some point, I realize it simply was not going to happen.

So, after a few years of frustration, in November 2015, I contacted the principal of the local high school. And wow what an awkward conversation that was! "Hey, so, the police think my father's killer was from the neighborhood, and thus, there's a good chance my father's killer attended your high school. Would you mind providing me five years of yearbooks for free so I can confirm this awful fact and bring ignominy to your lovely institution?" However, the principal was an absolute godsend, seemingly more willing to help confirm or deny the theory than the LAPD.

So, besides being a father, a husband, a son, a lawmaker, a constituent-services provider, and all the other things I tried to be, for a couple weeks, I sat down with post-it notes and pored over the yearbooks trying to find anyone who resembled the sketch. I then pored over the pictures to make sure. Next I tried googling those people: did anyone have a social-media profile that showed them living the "gangsta" life? Then I asked the two eyewitnesses to take a look at a few pictures, to see if it jogged any memories. Finally, I offered my concise report to the police on the most promising leads. "For what it's worth..."

I don't think they ever followed up.

MY FATHER'S BEST FRIEND

At some point, as part of my witness interviews, I reached out again to my father's closest local friend, a fellow about his same vintage who lived nearby, named Jim. The two old codgers would go antiquing together, and had become close in the years leading up to my dad's death, especially since my dad's elderly neighbor (and other close friend) had gotten dementia.

My father had relayed to Danielle and me that one of the reasons my he had been so upset with my sister Nicole's boyfriend, was that my father had asked Nicole to keep an eye on his house when he had traveled out of town one week, but she had allegedly delegated it to Mark, giving him the keys. My father, a private person, didn't like that at all. Moreover, he said he came home to find the automatic security light by his front door shattered. According to Jim, Mark had allegedly told my father that the light had gone on and Mark tried to adjust it with a stick, breaking it accidentally. Jim said he accompanied my dad to Home Depot to replace the light, right before my dad's death.

GIVE ME A SIGN

I'm not a superstitious man. I don't believe in astrology, dream interpretation, or Ouija boards. I don't believe in ghosts, unsettled spirits, or omens. I do believe generally in the power of prayer, but mostly either as a mantra or balm for the person praying. And yet despite my very rational, left-brained approach to things, over the course of the unsettling delay, I found myself thinking, "Dad, give me a sign!" Sometimes I would ask him to, directly. Sometimes I'd pray for it. Sometimes I would wonder if I needed to resuscitate the ancient practice of divining things from the flights of birds. This is how much the waiting game plays with your mind.

And the most frustrating thing is: no sign was forthcoming. My dad has not appeared to me in my dreams with a clue. No medium has contacted the police with a breakthrough. There has been no mystical guidance from the universe.

Some of you who believe in that stuff might be thinking that I'm just not trying hard enough, or looking in the right places. I will continue to believe in humanism, and that it's no aberration that no sign has come.

Some day, a person will solve this case using logic and evidence.

TOUGH DECISIONS

Toward the end of 2015, I had a decision to make. My tenure in the lower house would come to an end due to term limits the following year, in 2016. I could run for the State Senate in 2016 or run statewide in 2018. Either way, because of the hotly contested nature of political races in California, I had to make a decision soon. I was vexed. I believe I had a genuine gift for politics and was in it for the right reasons. Fifty-five measures I authored become law during my tenure, including landmark and much-needed reforms. I liked communicating with the media and the people to spread ideas that needed spreading, and I liked serving the greater good.

But since my dad's death, my heart wasn't in it. I spent much of my days and nights obsessing about solving the criminal case, or trying to deal with his messy civil affairs, and both were draining. I knew they were having an effect on my ability to do my job and to be a good father, two things that meant a lot to me.

For the first time, I was also mindful of my family's financial future. I had never cared much about money. Until recently I had driven a 1989 Chevy Caprice, which I had bought for $1000 or so. (When Danielle and I first met, and I pulled up in THAT, she considered for a moment whether I was an internet scammer because the car I drove was so out-of-place with my claimed station in life). I wore simple clothes and had simple tastes. I loved to travel, but other than that spent next to nothing. This frugality, plus lucky or well-timed investments, enabled me to run for office and not worry too much about my kids being able to afford Stanford. By 2012, I owned five properties.

But during my almost seven years in public office, I'd seen my family's net worth diminish, and the constant expenses related to my dad's case weren't helping. And now I learned there would be no relief coming. Instead of splitting my dad's estate three ways for the three siblings, or splitting it based on how many kids each sibling had (which is how my dad appeared to be re-crafting his estate plan when he died), my family was moving ahead with probating an outdated will.

We had a copy of my father's own words when he wrote that estate plan, decades ago. He had told his attorney that his son Michael was (then) an attorney at a big firm, (then) not married, and (then) with no kids, so Michael needed little or no help. But, he continued, his daughter Mariann, who had been a teen mother, (then) had fewer prospects for success (then), so needed more money. And that his other daughter, Nicole, who he was (then) close with, should handle the estate and get compensated for doing it.

It just goes to show how fast life could change. By the time my father died, I had become a public servant, with two children and hopefully more on the way. My sister Mariann had long since landed a good job, at a museum I helped create when I chaired a city commission, and she had become engaged to a wealthy investor. (I always thought my father's dated comments had sold her intellect and abilities short anyway, as both of my sisters are brilliant.) And from what he had told me, my father had not been getting along well with Nicole in the months before he died.

Nevertheless, those are the breaks.

My father had a decent middle-class estate. When he was murdered, he was in the process of reshaping his estate plans to skip a generation, that is, to pass his accumulated assets on to the children of his children only. Given that I had two children and Mariann one, his estate would have been divided 67% to my kids and 33% to her son.

My father had literally ordered change of beneficiary forms right before he was shot, and the overnight envelopes from his various banks were sitting in his house when we toured the crime scene. His new plans were found scattered around the same desk where he was found shot—but since he didn't sign and date those notes, they were not binding.

But with his old will still technically in place, his estate and all his accounts would be divided roughly / approximately 50% to Mariann, 36% to Nicole (largely in estate-management fees and the like), and 14% to me. In other words, as college funds go, my kids could not count on much from their Gramps.

And of course there was the criminal case. I've provided you a taste of the nonstop "tips" that came in. The ever-present need to fight for attention for what had become a cold case. The regular conversations with the investigations team. The re-interviewing witnesses. The obsessing. The concerns that despite what everyone thought, his murder might have something to do with my politics.

Considering all of these things, I decided not to run for the state senate in 2016. I was just going through too much. The thought briefly crossed my mind that if my dad's killing had something to do with my politics, I had let them win. But I put that aside and focused on pausing my political career so I could make money again, to take care of my family. A premature death in the family also gets you thinking: what will happen to them, if something happens to me? With very little getting passed on to them from my father, it was on me to make sure they had enough whenever I was gone.

For a few short months, the plan was to work during 2017, earn some decent money, and then run statewide in 2018. But in late 2016, Danielle surprised me with the news that she was pregnant with a boy—something we had been trying for, for years. With a third child on the way—and a due date during what would have been campaign season—and with nothing whatsoever resolved in my father's case—I decided to do the right thing for all who mattered to me, and pause my political career for the time being.

THREE YEARS,
IN THE BLINK OF AN EYE

November 2016 was, of course, the three-year anniversary. My office helped put on a large event for the families of murder victims. I spoke there, and I tried to comfort the families in attendance, and let them know that one policymaker at least, shared in their grief. Another speaker was Debra Tate, sister of Sharon Tate, murdered by the Manson gang. I remember asking myself, I wonder if my pain and anger will still be so raw after all those years go by.

A LOCAL PAPER

On February 1, 2016, the Los Feliz Ledger (a now defunct newspaper that had a circulation of 100,000 and covered the Los Angeles neighborhoods of Hollywood Hills, Los Feliz, and Silver Lake) reported that my older sister Nicole married her boyfriend a few hours before my father was murdered, in a private ceremony with no family members present.

SUICIDE?

In January 2017, a reporter let me know that a neighbor of my father's (one of the few who did not know him well) had told the reporter that he thought my father committed suicide. When pressed, he said, "well, when I saw him walking around the lake, he always had his head down and he looked sad." My father was just deep in thought when he walked. He did not commit suicide.

Nevertheless, when a murder is unsolved, the family of the victim often find themselves having to prove a negative or discuss yet another wild theory. This was one of those times.

ARMENIAN GANGS?

The ethnic breakdown of my district was roughly as follows. About 50% Anglo White. 20% Asian American, mostly of Filipino and Korean descent. 20% Hispanic. 15% Armenian American. Everyone else was represented in pretty small numbers. I liked to quip after my first campaign that it showed how Americans could all come together because these very disparate groups had elected the Italian in the race. But there had been some acrimony with one faction of the Armenian American community, who felt like the district was theirs. Because it contained both Glendale and East Hollywood, my district contained the greatest concentration of Armenian Americans anywhere. The militance from this one faction was strident, and my staff and I were occasionally subject to threats.

I had heard whispers that there was some connection, and in the early days after the murder, especially considering he had recently witnessed that faction committing some pretty serious voter fraud in a local council race, the thought certainly crossed my mind. Continuing my pattern of presenting everything to the detectives and letting them evaluate it, I had shared my thoughts with them. They were very dismissive.

It was thus jarring in Spring 2017 to receive what appeared to be very specific intelligence on this precise topic. Specifically, a local resident had emailed a local reporter, writing:

The only difference is that when you called me about the Gatto story my research led to a very dangerous local gang and Tamar indicated that we need to keep hands off and that you should be warned that there are rumors about the gang and the murder. . . . Because you mentioned the ethnicity of the suspect (I actually thought it was more than one) and my research also led in that direction I felt that for your safety I had to tell you. . . . In all fairness I actually did get quite paranoid about my family after Tamar and I discussed the realities of the gangs and she insisted I stay away from it all and she wanted you to know that the Gatto story is very sensitive to some in Little Armenia.

The reporter asked me for a comment. I was dumbfounded. Here was a guy professing specific knowledge about my father's case. I had no comment. I immediately e-mailed the detective and passed along this lead. I insisted on a call to discuss it. And I immediately e-mailed eight different Armenian friends of mine, who were immensely well-connected in the community. All of them reassured me that they had not heard anything like that, or really much at all.

The detectives were also fairly adamant that this was a false lead. They told me they had contacted the guy who sent the email, and he changed his tune a bit. While the text above could be read reasonably to indicate that he had received tips and pursued them further, and that those tips led him to others who confirmed it, and that he was scared for his safety—he presented a different picture when interviewed by the cops. He stated his only research had been googling Armenian gangs after being prompted to do so by the description he had read from the woman who confronted the car burglar. And that his references to sensitivity and safety pertained to the newspaper's relationships with the community. He did not want it losing readers or advertisers, he said, because it unfairly tarred a community sensitive and sadly accustomed to such accusations. After re-reading his entire e-mail, I acknowledged that this take could be consistent.

However, it still nagged at me. What if he simply told the police something different because he really did have specific intelligence and feared for his safety? So I pressed the police on this. I could tell I annoyed them pretty badly. They just did not believe the killer to be of Armenian heritage. Finally, one detective blurted out on a call, "Look—we have so many wires up in the Armenian community—we have so many snitches—we have so many suspects looking for shorter sentences. If there was any information, we'd have it."

Let's just say again that I and the detectives have different approaches to resolving unknowns. For me, the most important trait in such circumstances is *humility*. It's like that old proverb—if you're fumbling around in the dark, and you hear a large animal nearby, and you grab onto something long and kind of floppy— and you confidently proclaim "don't worry, I'll keep holding it, it's just an elephant's trunk"—you will be pretty upset when you learn it's a male donkey.

In sum, I recognize that this lead was probably nothing, and that the police probably had their reasons to be so confident. But whenever you have a lack of data, you must consider just about everything—lest you find out too late that you're holding onto the wrong preconceptions, which makes you, and what you're holding, a dick.

ITALIAN ORGANIZED CRIME?

On June 29, 2017, I received a call from a gentleman in Portland, Oregon. He stated that my father's murder was related to the recent murder of Phillip Anthony Gatto Jr., 57-years-old, in Oregon, who had been shot in a home-invasion robbery. The caller told me that both Phillip Gatto and my father were part of the same Italian organized-crime family.

I dutifully passed this lead onto the detectives too—mostly so if they got the same tip they didn't feel I was holding anything back. Perhaps some family members of mine have not always been on the up-and-up. But my father was not one of them, and had nothing to hide. I didn't know this Phillip Gatto, neither did my father, and to the best of my knowledge, he was not a relative. (I later learned he was perhaps—perhaps—a very distant cousin).

In any event, it later came out that Phillip Gatto was a prominent cocaine dealer. The only things my father trafficked in were garage-sale finds.

MURDER FOR HIRE?

In September 2017, the Los Angeles Times and the Chicago Tribune reported how a local businessman had allegedly ordered three hits, two in the Los Angeles area, and then fled to Montenegro. Other than involving another sordid murder, something in the stories caught my eye. The mastermind had allegedly used a hitman for hire in each killing, and the sketch that law enforcement released roughly resembled the sketch in my father's case.

As I often remarked, my father's case was either really simple—a case of horrible bad luck—or it was something vastly more complicated: a staged crime scene and a murder for hire.

The problem is, if you stare at enough sketches of generic-looking criminals in hoodies (the hitman in the other case was a young white male who wore a hoody, but then how common is wearing a hoody?)—they all start to resemble one another.

Still, I passed this onto the police. Or perhaps the right phrase is: I annoyed them with yet another theory.

MY MOM

At some point in the course of all the discussions, I had a reporter ask me—or more accurately express a theory—about whether my mom was involved. Although this was no laughing matter, I almost guffawed. My mother, 71-years-old at the time of my father's passing, weighs 99 pounds, volunteers at her church and the Assistance League, and is the most kind and gentle person I know. And I'm not just saying that because she's my mother. The word people who know her most often use to describe her is, "saint."

My mother has the personality of the character Melanie Hamilton Wilkes in *Gone with the Wind*. You know, the nice blonde who serves as a contrast to Scarlett O' Hara. She's gracious, graceful, and kind, almost to the point of being timid. And she's devoutly Catholic, obtaining a papal annulment instead of a divorce from my father, when they split after 24 years of marriage. When my mom heard my father was murdered, she cried and cried. Despite having their differences, she loved him, and bore him three children.

So although I was shocked when asked, I tried to be patient with the reporter.

After we hung up, I paused, quietly for a moment, and reflected on what my life had become. Answering patently absurd questions about whether my elderly mother—the kindest human I know—could have been involved in my father's murder.

AN UNINVITED GUEST?

Shortly after the Los Feliz Ledger story, I was asked to lunch by a retired male journalist who also lived in the Silver Lake neighborhood. He shared with me a theory that up until that point, I had not heard from anyone else. He said he rejected the notion that the car burglar had anything to do with it. He echoed the idea that everyone was probably reading way too much into it, and that it was likely just a coincidence—someone breaking into cars in a big city, which occurs daily. He also rejected the idea that the killing was something very complicated, one of the more nefarious plots that some people were floating.

Instead he proposed a hybrid theory. Presumably, my sister and her boyfriend had told several people that they were getting married that day, as well as a few business associates, perhaps a caterer, a flower provider, et cetera. His theory was that the killer was someone who learned about their wedding and expecting that my father would be at the wedding, naturally, had decided to burgle his unattended home. But then my father surprised him, and he freaked out, and shot him. Who would have thought a father would *not* be at his daughter's wedding?

I could not argue with his logic. Of all the various theories, some wilder than others, this one could not be ruled out. It synthesized the "people don't just enter inhabited dwellings" weak points of the "car burglar" theory with the "your dad likely surprised this person" angle, all the while giving significance to the big coincidence that the paper had reported recently.

MORE FALSE LEADS

In mid-2017, I read on Nextdoor how an auto burglar was taken into custody near my dad's old neighborhood. This particular fellow was in his early twenties, mid height, and breaking into cars fairly brazenly at midday, while wearing a hoodie. Now while I know this general description and circumstances probably describes tens of thousands of petty criminals, I got excited because in the pictures posted, he also looked just like the sketch in my dad's case. I emailed the detective who brought this new suspect into custody. The detective replied that the perpetrator was booked for a misdemeanor only (a troubling new trend in LA) and therefore not swabbed for DNA. I asked the detectives on my dad's case to question him though, to see if he was part of an auto burglary ring, or if he knew something. I don't think it ever happened. And I'm sure they didn't like me telling them how to do their job. No one does. But I couldn't help myself. A lead was a lead.

Also in 2017, I was contacted by a D-List actress who had attended my father's school and who knew him well. She found me on Twitter and sent me a DM. She was charming and reasonably successful. Will you have lunch with me, she asked, so I can share with you a hot tip on your father's death? Naturally, I said yes. She had known him for decades, and perhaps knew something.

I wasn't prepared for the special brand of crazy this episode would be. She was in a huge battle with her ex and tried to tell me that he had some involvement. Why, I asked? I could understand maybe giving this theory some credence if my father had been sleeping with this actress, but that was not the case. Over the course of a long lunch, she spun a meandering and I must say, "out-there" theory involving the Clintons, my father, her ex, and her tweets. If I understood it correctly—and it was VERY hard to follow—she had tweeted that she was going to Silver Lake around the time of my father's murder, and thus, her ex had assumed she was visiting my father (who as far I as I knew, had been her teacher decades before, and that's all), and that she knew stuff about the Clintons and her ex knew that, so decided to kill my dad as a warning. It was, put charitably, crazy talk. My assessment was that she was not onto something, but that she was on something.

As I departed the lunch and had some time to reflect on the way home, I remember thinking about how my hope—that someone finally had a lead worth exploring that would break the case open—had been turned into bitter anger, at wasted time, and yet another attempt for me to bring down the law on someone a tipster disliked. Damn these people for toying with emotions. I wonder if they understood how cruel their actions were.

MORE DISCUSSIONS AND CLUES

Throughout 2016 and 2017, as the different theories and tips came in, I continued to have regular discussions with the detectives. For example, in the middle of 2016, they told me that 102 tips and leads had come in, but that they had stopped. It appears that the public's attention span was about two and a half years.

They told me my father's backdoor was found unlocked, but this is likely because whoever was in the house had time to fetch the garden shears from his backyard.

They told me that the perpetrator had time to open about thirty jewelry envelopes in my father's room.

And they finally confirmed that they did not give too much credence to the sketch.

Of course, the lack of progress meant that no one had talked, no one had snitched, no one had re-offended. One of our calls concluded with that depressing note. "All the normal things that help a case get solved are just not happening."

A JOYOUS DAY

In June 2017, my son was born. Joseph Michael Gatto. I named him after my father. He was a fighter from the moment of his birth. He was premature. One (perhaps clueless or dramatic) nurse initially told me it looked bad, based on his lack of responsiveness. But after just two nights in the Intensive Care Unit, he came home.

Being a large Italian family, we have a lot of Josephs, Joes, and Joeys. So everyone just started calling him Jack. And after about a year, Jack sprouted yellow-blond hair, which he still has. But despite these differences, there is no mistaking it: there is much of my father in him.

My father used to rise in the morning and eat a raw tomato—a practice that Jack started doing with no prodding, as a toddler. My father loved fruit trees. So does Jack. He insisted I plant him a mulberry tree, and gorges on any fresh fruit he can find. He has some of the same mannerisms of my father, and the same sense of humor. Jack is the greatest son a father could ask for.

Jack provides me untold joy every day. But sometimes when I think about things, I can't help being a little sad that my dad never got a chance to meet his namesake. Because he would have loved this kid. Jack is a smart, funny, mischievously charming little cuss— instantly the "mayor" of any room he enters. My dad would have loved watching him play T-ball and football, and would have chuckled at how Italian in spirit this little blond kid is.

Although Jack knows of him only in stories about "Gramps", we try to keep my father's memory alive in all of our children, even Jack.

RAGE AT THE MEDIA

As the time passed and none of the leads panned out, many people started to question the police's dominant consensus, that this crime was a random / freak occurrence by a stupid criminal. I must have had a hundred people tell me things like, "stupid criminals brag. Young criminals re-offend. How has this not occurred here?" I must have had a further hundred people tell me that some enormous percentage of elderly people who are murdered are murdered by someone they know. Moreover, the crime—so out of place—had rocked my father's close-knit, quiet neighborhood. So in addition to the oddball tips, I certainly heard my share of simple frustration at the lack of answers, from people who knew and cared about my dad.

Several members of the media were kind enough to keep my father's story alive. They would dutifully cover the vigils, the memorials, the anniversaries, the requests for help from the public. These included a variety of broadcast reporters like Robert Kovacik, as well as print journalists at every local paper.

One print journalist was particularly interested in my father's killing, because she happened to attend the same church he did. She submitted a variety of questions to the detectives over the years. Almost all the time, they were met with pushback, stonewalling, and a strange rage. On two separate occasions, one of the detectives on my father's case—Mr. Bedside Manner himself, said things like, "if you talk to that fucking bitch, tell her she's not going to get anything." I can't tell you how off-putting this was. You have to understand he was spitting mad, and "bitch" was one of several choice words he used.

Don't get me wrong, certain things the media requested I didn't necessarily feel great about. I'm not sure my family was ready to see crime-scene photos, for example. I'm not sure the gory details of the autopsy would be pleasant to read. But this detective wasn't pushing back to protect my family. It was simply parochialism and annoyance: protecting his domain and not wanting extra work. She had rubbed him the wrong way, and I got a sense he wasn't a big fan of strong women to begin with. These ongoing battles—and his ongoing rage toward her, was frustrating.

It was also stupid. When you're the family of a murder victim, you desperately don't want your case to be forgotten. And in a case like this (young dude, running through the neighborhood), you never know when someone will say, "hey I know that guy." In sum:

you want all the help you can get, and the media is a powerful force for good in these cases. The detective didn't view things that way. He viewed any second guessing as an attack on the job he was doing. This was unfortunate and counterproductive.

I think about all the families of murder victims who hire a high-profile attorney and hold news conferences to question the job the police are doing. With my position and my many friends in the media, I could have done this in a heartbeat, and gotten twenty cameras there. But I never did. Even though many people suggested it, I refrained. I knew the department wanted my dad's case solved, and I respected the folks in the department who were working so hard on the case.

But why the detectives would be so hostile toward mere media interest in a case like this was troubling. I also believe their actions with this reporter violated our unwritten agreement. The family never criticized them—didn't even vent our frustration publicly—but, we expected them to at least answer our questions and allow the media to do its job: help publicize the case and the reward, and manifest the collective curiosity of their readers regarding the tragic death of a beloved community fixture.

There are so many caring people in law enforcement, who got in it and stay in it for the right reason, because they want to help people. Most detectives who work on murder cases fall in that category. I encountered a lot of that kindly attitude and approach both within the LAPD and outside, from the many folks in law enforcement who contacted me to offer help. However, I was starting to think that some of the team on my father's case wasn't great.

OF STRs AND SURNAMES

Since my father's death, I had immersed myself in the world of genetic genealogy. I had done so for two reasons: First, I had read about its promise to solve crimes, and I wanted to be able to speak the language if I had questions for the detectives. Second, I had to patch some holes in my family tree. When a loved one dies suddenly, you don't get to ask them the questions you wanted to before they passed—and I had several about my own family that I couldn't ask my dad anymore.

I read everything I could get my hands on—and this was dense, hard-to-understand stuff.

The most fascinating and promising concept I learned about were how Short Tandem Repeats on the Y-Chromosome could be used as a sort of genetic surname. How? Well, males inherit their Y-Chromosome more or less unchanged from their father, generation after generation. Minor mutations occur, and that is how you can trace a line of descent and often, the movement of peoples. On the Y Chromosome are certain Short Tandem Repeats, or STRs. These are short sequences of DNA, normally 2-5 base pairs in length, that are repeated numerous times. At one location, a male might have 13 repeats. At another, he may have 25. All are within a range, and the ranges are well known.

Taken together, this sequence of numbers is not that different from a bar code. Each male lineage has its own unique bar code. Many of these bar codes are specific even to a surname. And they can further indicate where someone's male line originated in the world.

In this era of genetic genealogy, the internet is full of web pages by amateur genetic genealogists, called, "projects," where they publish their STR sequences and try to connect with other relations. For example (and I'm borrowing this example from the *Da Vinci Code*), you might see a page that reads like this. "Welcome to the Sinclair Surname Project. Here, we ask all males with the Sinclair surname or a variant to post their STRs as tested by a major lab, to determine if and whether we are related. It is believed that most Sinclair males, although from England, originated in Normandy, France, where the surname was originally St. Clair…."

Now I know the limitations of using DNA that comes from just one parent. For example, if you only had Barack Obama's maternal DNA, you would only connect it to a white family—and that would be deeply misleading if you were trying to figure out his appearance. I also grasp that out-of-wedlock births occur, and not everyone with a surname is really descended from a male with that surname.

However, after years of no breakthroughs, why wouldn't we want to try this method? Who wouldn't we want to see if we got lucky? The payoff could be great.

If the killer's STR sequence matched that posted on a public page of the O'Neill family (to pick one of several such pages online), the cops could look for O'Neills that lived in the area and met the general description. Again, assuming the murderer was not one of the small percentages of kids born out of wedlock, this would be a huge lead.

It could also help inform our outreach, because we might get lucky another way. If the STR sequence didn't reveal any surname leads, but it indicated that the killer was likely of Uzbek heritage, I would be rather upset that the police and I had confine our outreach to the English-speaking media, and we could adjust accordingly.

I mentioned these concepts at least four times to the detectives. At first, it was clearly apparent that they just didn't understand. These were detectives, not DNA lab technicians. I didn't expect them to understand. I worked at explaining things better.

The second time, they mumbled something about not having time. I told them that I would get volunteers to do this. They said no. They could not release evidence to a volunteer. (As far as I know, the LAPD is different from other departments, which use volunteer genealogists all the time.) I also questioned whether this is really accurate. A string of STRs looks something like this: DYS391: 15. If they asked folks to search the internet to look for a certain pattern, they wouldn't have to say why—the main research here would be to locate the public webpages that displayed *their* evidence, for the whole world to see.

The third time, they mumbled something about not wanting to wade into ethnic issues. I get that, kind of. I didn't see how this would be different from describing a suspect as a "Caucasian male, possibly of Russian heritage." And again, it could bear serious fruit and help us narrow down our outreach and searches.

I want to stress that this is not like the police searching entire genomes on 23andMe or Ancestry.com, and trying to find a killer based on who he is related to. (We'll get to that concept later). It is also not the same as looking for male relatives who have been convicted of a crime.

This is literally comparing a bunch of very specific numbers on one chromosome to public projects that say, "most men with the surname Bogonovic have this pattern, and are of Bosnian heritage. . ." Either data point could break the case open.

At some point, after all the confusion and pushback, I just put this aside for the time being.

MORE TIPS

Around this time, I received another "great tip," this time from a Facebook friend, whose brother attended the same high school I did, although later. She sent me a link to an article, about some young people, ages 19-20, who were arrested for killing someone with a car accidentally, while driving intoxicated in the San Fernando Valley. She was sure they had a connection to my father's death.

You have to understand how people word these tips. They don't just lead with the craziness. They usually start with an innocuous and promising message, to get your attention, and get you talking to them. Then, they dribble out the information. When you finally find out that they are under the influence of a substance or in need of psychological help, you've already wasted a lot of time and heartache.

When I kept probing how this woman knew these young people were involved with my dad's death, she finally told me: she had had a dream that they were.

Now, I thought, trying to keep hope alive despite what my brain was telling me—OK, maybe she doesn't want to put in writing that she has some kind of insider knowledge—maybe she doesn't want to snitch on them that directly. I got sucked in—"when did you have this dream." "1987" was her response.

I couldn't help myself this time—I had to clarify. "So, you had a dream in 1987 about people who weren't born yet—that they were going to kill my father 25 years in the future—a man who you hadn't met yet?" Yes, was her response.

The more she said, the more it became apparent that this was just another mentally unbalanced person, with little concern for how difficult these communications were on a victim's family member, me.

I also figured—if they were indeed arrested for felony vehicular manslaughter, they'll get swabbed for DNA, and the system will take care of everything else.

A BITTERSWEET VISIT TO ITALY

My father loved traveling to Italy. Italian was his first language, but he had to re-learn it as an adult. As a child in a Colorado steel town, he had been beaten for speaking it at school, so like most immigrant families of his generation, they worked to assimilate. Still, my father was emphatically Italian. Both as a young boy and teenager, he bore a striking resemblance to the main character in *Cinema Paradiso*. And the hometowns of our ancestors were not that different from the small town depicted in that movie.

In 2018, I got a call from the Mayor of my paternal grandfather's small town, high in the mountains of Cosenza province. They were naming a street after my father. Would I come to the ceremony?

I loved visiting my grandfather's hometown, and had been there twice before. The people, though mostly poor, were smart, worldly, and welcoming. Very isolated, the mountain dwellers there are descendants of ancient Italic tribes and Roman settler stock.

I also felt a special closeness to them because of our traditions. My father had instilled in me a keen sense of empathy with the unfortunate and the downtrodden: immigrants, refugees, and those who the powerful picked on. Although Cosenza was so isolated—and isolation often produces great prejudice and xenophobia, for some reason, Cosenza was always welcoming to those in need. The values I inherited from my father were part of the tradition in Cosenza that had been passed on for centuries.

In the 12th Century, an ascetic proto-Protestant movement emerged in France and Switzerland, called the Waldensians. They preached a simple life, and rejected formal Catholic dogma, for which they were declared heretics. Several countries in Europe subjected them to horrible persecutions. But the people of Cosenza welcomed the Waldensian refugees, and to this day there are still pockets that speak Occitan instead of Italian. The Waldensians would suffer greatly when the Spanish took over Cosenza and implemented the Inquisition.

In the 15th Century, Turkish Muslim raiders took over what is now Albania, and subjected the local population to horrible depredations. Many Albanians fled and became refugees, but they weren't always accepted in Western Europe because they practiced a type of Eastern Orthodox Christianity. But Cosenza welcomed the refugees, and to this day there are still many towns that speak Arbëreshë, which is Albanian with an Italian twist. Regis Philbin was the descendant of these Albanian refugees who settled in Cosenza.

And during World War II, the Nazi occupiers located a concentration camp for Jews and others in Cosenza, called Ferramonti. The locals refused to accept the harsh paradigm that marked other camps. Throughout the duration of the war, they interacted with and socialized with the inmates, even taking the children out for gelato. When the Nazis were losing control of Italy and tried to deport the inmates to Aushwitz, the Cosenza authorities simply "lost" the orders. Thus, Ferramonti was the only concentration camp in Europe to book just four deaths for the entire duration of the war, and those were by natural causes. The people of Cosenza were the only people in Europe to stand up for humanity in this manner.

As we made the long drive from Tuscany to Cosenza, I thought about how my family's traditions and experiences had made me who I am. And how the transmission mechanism for those traditions, my father, was now gone. Unable to tell me any more family history. Unable to pass on recipes and holiday rituals. Unable to be here for the naming of a street in his father's hometown.

The visit was nevertheless joyful. The street-naming ceremony was wonderful. I gave a speech in broken Italian, that I had composed with the help of Google translate. My children got to see window into how their great-grandfather had lived.

And we surprised my father's first cousin, Diana—heck every visit to her was a surprise, because she didn't have a computer, a cell phone, or even an answering machine. (And she only spoke dialect, and with my poor Italian, I never even bothered *trying* to call her!) But we were pleased to find that nothing had changed. We knocked on her door, and she gave us a big hug, and welcomed us in for a fantastic home-cooked meal.

The last time we had seen her, she had teased Danielle and I to bring back a boy. And we did. As she held my son, tears welled up in her vivid blue eyes.

PRIVATE DETECTIVE

In 2018, I was mindful that November that year would mark five years with no breakthrough. I had tried everything. Pursued every lead. My assessment of the LAPD at that point was frankly mixed. After connecting with other family members of murder victims, I knew that smaller police departments provided more dedicated investigations and worked more closely with family members. Some of this is only natural. If there are two murders in some small city, and one of them goes unsolved, the police force there takes it as a stain on a perfect record. Los Angeles will never be that city. Los Angeles had more than a murder a day in 2021. But Los Angeles' size also worked to its advantage. It had larger teams, bigger budgets, and better technology. Those qualities were hard for smaller cities to match.

The culture in the LAPD has come under fire from various places over the last thirty years. I for one believe the average police officer genuinely cares about doing good, and putting bad people behind bars. I've never been a supporter of the ill-conceived slogan, "defund the police." But I had my own gripes with the LAPD culture at times.

It most often came after I read about some small city where some retired detective was poring over some cold case, and then reached out to some DNA expert or another volunteer outsider, who worked on the case with the creative obsession that only a wonk would bring. Some days, after chatting with the cops, I got a sense that they were just waiting for a DNA hit—and not doing the extra stuff that outsiders could perhaps help with. I want to stress that I don't blame them for not having the time. I realize the detectives, particularly the elite ones, get called off any one case all the time—since there is always a high-profile case in Los Angeles, always another murder.

Still, the LAPD had been publicly criticized for its approach to handling murder cases, particularly ones with DNA evidence. The documentary "Tales of the Grim Sleeper" questioned why it took the police thirty years to solve that crime. I had heard from dozens of families of murder victims (at marches and rallies and the like) about their bad experiences with the LAPD. Again, I dismissed much of this, willing to give them the benefit of the doubt always—because I understood that *any* unsolved murder is frustrating.

But I had still been troubled by some of the things. It wasn't just the poor bedside manner and cluelessness that makes a detective lecture a grieving family member—literally with tears still in his eyes—about legislation. It wasn't the odd outbursts for the behavior of a second cousin once removed as a 14-year-old. It was mainly the hostility toward my *questions* and the rage toward a well-meaning journalist. I was treated like an *intrusion*—a nuisance—even when I pointed out valid things that the police ended up thanking me for later. This included telling them about an item in the house they had forgotten to fingerprint, and helping with everything from accessing my father's computer equipment to getting the DNA uploaded into familial DNA. They say sometimes that the archetypal cop personality lacks interpersonal sensitivity. But I also found them at times lacking scientific curiosity.

By the end of 2017, I had worn out my welcome with the detectives. My emails asking for updates received curt replies, like, "there are no new leads." My discussions of the case with their political or departmental bosses—which 90% of the time were prompted not by me—had resulted in unwanted pressure on them, not of my doing.

In sum, I was having all sorts of negative feelings about the investigation. And I believe negative emotions are a call to action. So in early 2018, I decided to hire a private detective. Despite the warnings that it would piss off the detectives—cops are notoriously territorial and resistant of non-police outsiders interfering with an investigation and trying to take the glory—I was finally in that, "what do you have to lose" stage that makes family members of murder victims resort to psychics and/or private detectives. Not one to go the psychic route, I hired a private detective who had contacted me to offer his services, one who knew my sisters too.

After a few months of investigations and discussions, he said he felt like there were many holes in the investigation, and came up with a list of several questions to ask the investigators.

A WRENCH IN THE TIMELINE?

The private detective immediately proved his value because he put in shoe leather, and actually discovered something that might inform the case. How? He went around my father's neighborhood and talked with his neighbors. One would think this occurred extensively around the time of his murder, and some of it surely had, but there were also neighbors who had simply not been interviewed. Including one with an important clue.

If you stood on my father's front porch and threw a baseball, you'd hit his across the street neighbors, who lived in a fairly small house on his tiny street. Directly behind them (still within baseball throwing distance) was another woman whose address was on another street, but whose property was quite close as the crow flies to my father.

She was adamant that at 6:20pm that evening, *i.e.*, when my father should have been home from Costco already, but *before* the car-burglar interactions occurred, she heard one very loud pop that sounded like a firecracker going off. This being almost five years after the fact of course, I was particularly concerned with validating her memory. Two things provided instant credibility. One, she was so concerned about her safety, that she hit the deck and crawled around for a while. She furthermore called a neighbor and inquired whether her adolescent had set off a firecracker or fired a gun. The fact that she hit the deck makes me think that she credibly was scared about her safety. The next step was verifying her timeline. How could she be sure this occurred when she said it did? She had an answer for that as well. Every night, she took her son to an extracurricular activity, and had to leave the house at precisely 6:30pm. She was positive this occurred while she was getting ready to leave. Thus, her timeframe was also credible.

If the noise she heard was indeed the gunshot, it of course had the potential for changing the focus of the investigation. It might mean that the focus on the car burglar was simply misplaced. It might mean that he was still involved, but that he was in my father's home before he broke into cars (which would be even weirder). It could mean that he was indeed a decoy. It could mean that he fired the gun at someone or something else. Or it could have just been a coincidence: a backfire, a truck dropping something heavy, or some kid playing with fireworks.But either way, I could not believe that we were learning this, five years after the fact.

When I spoke with the detectives about it, they followed up. But they concluded that it just couldn't have been relevant, because it "it would be impossible given what is known about what your dad did [meaning working on his website or reading emails] for this to work out in the existing time frame." Mind you, to this day I am unsure of the details or what this meant. If my father's clocks were not set properly, and were just an hour off, it would presumably mean that the neighbor's timeline did in fact fit. I do not know if they verified the timeline on servers, or just with his local equipment. Moreover, if the perpetrator or perpetrators were interested in what was on his computers, it could have been someone else moving the mouse.

MORE HOLES

This was just one of several concerns I had after seeing the private detective's report. I decided I owed it to my father to raise the rest of them too. Heck, maybe the detectives would appreciate a new perspective, as certainly some of the issues would add value. But I realized this was probably fantasy, and thus I had some concern before e-mailing them because I knew it could also be interpreted as questioning their investigation. Plus for certain of the questions, I already knew the answer: the detectives had not done the right thing. Below are excerpts of my e-mail.

First, I tried to soften the blow:

First, in the interest of full disclosure, I should tell you that I hired a private-eye firm to help me think through all angles and leads. Permission to speak directly and candidly: I know that sometimes police detectives get offended when someone hires some non-police private-eye to help out. Please don't be. I know you guys have busted your humps on this.

As you guys have seen, as the most public face of the family, I receive many "leads" and "tips"—some wacky and some that require follow-through and time. I always pass them along to you, but it will help my peace of mind to have a private-eye talk things through with me.

Then I made the following queries:

- When they got the phone records from all the people in my father's life, from my sisters' boyfriends to my dad's gardener—did they get just phone calls and text messages, or did they get iMessages too? (iMessages are entirely different—carriers don't log them or even receive them.) With almost everyone having an iPhone, how could they rule out someone sending a message, "it's done" without getting everyone's iMessages?

- Were there any cell-phone-related leads at all from people who connected to towers close by on the day of the incident? Did they pursue this at all?

- Were there fingerprints on the car that matched prints in my dad's house? Because if not, then we were likely barking up the wrong tree. And if the perp wore gloves one place and not the other, it seems a lot more professional than it may seem.

- Had they tried to determine whether my father's safes had been opened by anyone before the murder, and whether there were any prints on items inside?

- Did they ever try to account for all keys to his house? Who had them, and where were they now?

- Why hadn't they interviewed several of the people who knew my dad well? I detailed for them the half-dozen people who had contacted me with this same question, and offering information. This included neighbors, close family members, and close friends. Even if they were trying to resolve basic questions that the kids might not know, like, "did your father ever meet women online?"—some of his friends may know this.

- Finally, I renewed my request for them to ask everyone in my father's close circle—not just family members, but friends, key vendors, etc.—to take polygraph tests.

In total, I asked them nineteen questions. While I never presumed to know their business better than them, certainly some of these were valid questions, and a couple of them were clear oversights. I thought, all things considered, I was behaving nicely. Unlike families of other prominent crimes, I wasn't holding weekly press conferences or anything criticizing the investigation.

Yet they responded to my valid questions with an exceedingly curt email. They said, in sum: piss off, we're not answering any more of your annoying questions. But since *one* of your questions requested polygraphs, let's start with you and your wife, asshole.

POLYGRAPH

"No problem!" I replied. "I'm happy to lead by example and go first, so no one else in my dad's circle feels picked on. When do you want me there?"

On the appointed day, I showed up for my polygraph test.

It went a lot stranger than I thought it would. They left me in the room for long periods, and while they were gone, I opened my briefcase and did work. They came back and told me that was not allowed. I had to sit quietly. OK. I didn't see the purpose of this, except to annoy me.

Then the detectives left and an examiner came in. He was one of the biggest jerks I ever met, and that says a lot. But I'm sure part of it was his job.

He started by asking me all these really stupid questions. "Do you always tell the truth?" I guess most people in such situations say, "yes." But I know that this is logically one of those questions that is counterintuitive. Since no one always tells the truth, the person who says they do is lying. And the person who says that they lie sometimes is telling the truth. I answered honestly. "No." He was taken aback—what do you mean? I said, "well, if my wife isn't wearing a particularly flattering outfit, I don't always blurt that out. Moreover, in politics, I hear lots of stupid ideas for legislation every day, but I tell people I respect their ideas…."

He then said, "well, do you always follow the law?" To that I also said, "no." He got downright pissed. Again I sensed that most everyone here deluded themselves, and that he needed that to do his test. But I made a commitment to be honest, and honest I would be. "What do you mean?" he said. "Well, just the other day I left my wife's car in a loading zone when I checked my PO Box. That wasn't legal. And I don't always know if my tax deductions are proper but I take them anyway. Nothing major. But I can't look you in the eye and say, 'I always follow the law' or 'I'm a law-abiding person' because neither are technically true."

He got really upset, and it was very off-putting. He lectured me how it was troubling that I admitted these things so casually. All the while I was thinking, "gosh how troubling it is if people don't." He then basically said that we couldn't proceed and he would refuse to administer the test unless I gave him better answers.

What an awful thing to say. I think maybe he needed me to lie to him to calibrate something. But it's strange position to be in, since I came there resolved to tell the truth.

Next we did the test itself. He asked me all these run-on questions, with twists and turns, dependent clauses, and double negatives. These questions were in the vein of, "when you picture your father's murder, can you say positively that you have not failed to disclose anything from the police, which you may have known, but didn't share…"

I told him I had withheld certain things, but the detectives already knew it and why, and as far as I knew, agreed with my reasoning. Recall that I had my own personal notes, which I hadn't shared with anyone, for fear that their exhaustive and wide-ranging suspicions and theories could be used to acquit the real perpetrator someday. So, part of the day focused on this.

Then came the key part of every polygraph test—the third degree, while the subject is not hooked up to the machine. I knew nothing of polygraphs going in, but I later learned that these questions were the main part of the experience. Grilling the subject, trying to get them to break.

It's my understanding that a polygraph doesn't really tell if someone is lying; it provides indicia. Most of the value derives from making the subject *think* they screwed up, and then questioning them intensely, at which point many people get caught in a lie, or just spill the beans.

The examiner came at me with some wild stuff. "We know you needed campaign funds. So you sent someone over there to ask your dad for a contribution, and when things went wrong, your campaign worker killed him."

If the demeanor of the examiner wasn't so intensely assholish, I would have busted out laughing. I kept thinking, "this guy is yelling at me with a straight face, berating me, and yet, these guys don't do their research." A part of me grasped that they had to come at everyone with things like that to gauge reactions. And I suppose this was the best they could do in my case.

So while the experience would have been comic, it wasn't, because it was so awfully uncomfortable. You see, I have always been a pretty darn good political fundraiser. While many people believe you can never have enough money, I truly did not need any additions to my campaign warchest. As a plucky upstart given zero chance of winning, in my first campaign I had raised $1.4 million, with almost none of it coming from PACs. I was lucky to have so many supporters and true friends, who had each chipped in small amounts to get to that total.

At the time of my father's death, I held one of the most-powerful positions in the Capitol. So, raising money wasn't a problem. So to have this examiner screaming at me—literally like an officer in basic training hazes a plebe—that I had something to do with my father's death over a campaign contribution? It was truly bizarre!

But most of the questions focused on whether I was holding something back, i.e., to protect someone in the family. Later, I found it very ironic that while the police perhaps thought I was holding back to protect people, others felt I was spreading rumors to hurt them. I was doing neither; I was trying to walk the tightrope of making sure every lead was investigated, without having the police chase wild theories.

When I spoke with several of my friends in law enforcement after my long day was done, the consensus was clear: I had pissed off the detectives with pointing out ways they had not done their job correctly. I had further pissed them off by creating more work for them, by insisting that they polygraph a bunch of people. So they did something truly awful: they put me through it. They did it in the most bullying, awful, horrible way.

My trust for them evaporated. Doubly so when I found out that they never followed up to polygraph anyone else. This was clearly a message to me.

It's one you don't easily forget. To do this to a family member of a murder victim—for being insistent that they follow up on leads—was an awful thing to do. And in my eyes, it wasn't strike three—it was strike five. First the lecture on my politics as I grieved, then the bizarre asides about my cousin's behavior decades ago, then the constant misogyny toward the caring reporter, the hostility toward valid questions, and now this. This was an unprofessional crew who I no longer wanted on my dad's case.

And they had done this with the evil cleverness of veteran law enforcement experience, applied as a power move. They knew that as a politician, I couldn't hold a press conference and say, "they put me through a totally unnecessary polygraph because I asked them to follow up on leads"—because all they would need to do is put out an official statement, somber in its tone, and careful to imply just enough, "we followed up on a requested lead, and part of that was questioning Mr. Gatto…" Just enough to make the public doubt enough to ruin my career.

As I left that day, the detective who had always wanted a copy of my personal notes said to me, "well, things are going to change now—and that will include getting a copy of your papers."

I don't think I lost my dignity or my composure during the entire ordeal. But I lost my faith in the system.

A few months later, I heard that the two detectives had been pulled off my dad's case. I genuinely had nothing to do with it. Don't get me wrong, I had felt like telling the Mayor and the media what an awful human being one was, but had never done so. But I like to think that someone in the police department got their most report and had said, "you did WHAT?"

AN UNFORTUNATE PUBLIC SPAT

In Fall 2019, my sister Nicole submitted a request for over $600,000 in administrators' fees for herself and attorneys' fees for her lawyers. I found this excessive and hard to swallow. My father hated lawyers and bureaucracy, and would turn over in his grave to learn that his hard-earned money was being spent thusly.

But it was her self-serving declaration, filed with the request, that really bothered me. Her declaration accused me and my other sister Mariann (who I was also avoiding) of conspiring to make life difficult on Nicole by bringing suspicion on her. I was really upset. I didn't make up the facts of Nicole's life, nor did I publicize them.

As the public face of the family, I had fielded dozens of tips and entertained dozens of theories. I had told everyone not to rush to judgment. And I had asked the police to investigate every theory, no matter how painful they may be. What kind of son would I be if I didn't?

Specifically, I told the police several times that I wanted the investigation to go wherever it needed—even if that meant finding out that my father was killed by beloved actor Tom Hanks. I tried to share with the police everything—even crazy tips—and if anything, I had been put through the ringer because the police felt like I was *holding back* my notes that included salacious details about my family.

So when I read her filing, I was deeply saddened. But I also knew as a lawyer that dysfunction between business associates or family members can often result in the unfortunate situation of people communicating through court filings. So, for the first time in the case, I broke my silence on this topic. My integrity means the world to me. So I had to refute the notion that the suspicions were anything other than her own doing.

I had carefully avoided any public discussion of intra-familial squabbles. And it was heartbreaking for me to see this family feud spill over in the media, but it did. One such story, in The Eastsider, stated plainly: "Gatto was considering disinheriting his daughter Nicole, the executor of his estate, and re-writing his will in the months before his death, according to [a] review of the documents." The story also referred to my father's own words, gleaned from his own e-mails, to various parties, that were submitted to the court.

The media stories also featured another part of the case that had absolutely broken my heart, something I had also not talked about much. My father was very close with legendary craftsman Sam Maloof. Maloof made gorgeous furniture with gorgeous wood, all without metal screws. If you don't know about the beauty of his pieces, I suggest looking him up.

Sometime in the early 1970s, Sam Maloof had given my father a cradle hutch. All of us kids had slept in it. The hutch was giant—about seven and a half feet tall. And it was beautiful and rare. It is my understanding that two similar pieces existed—one was given by Maloof to President Jimmy Carter; the other was in the Smithsonian.

And it was also sentimental. People have written thousands of poignant words on how much an heirloom can mean to a family. This one meant a lot to my father and me. When I started having kids, my father tearfully gave the piece to me. You must understand, above all, he wanted it to be enjoyed and for the family heirloom to stay in the family. I was the only child of his who was procreating. Mariann, who had gotten pregnant at 14 and born a child at 15, was done. Nicole, now beyond childbearing age, had never begun. I had two, on my way to three.

The irony in all this is that I had asked my father to keep the cradle for us at his house. The piece was way too tall for the ceilings in our tiny Los Angeles home, and I didn't want to ship the precious piece to our temporary Sacramento abode—it would have cost a fortune and risked damaging it. I never thought my father would die suddenly, and I never thought my ownership would be in doubt. I told my father we'd use it when we were over at his house (which we did), and that I could pick it up when we moved into a larger house someday.

At the time, I was in no rush. I was not done having kids. My father was in great shape—I never expected him to die, and I never expected anyone to lie about what we all knew.

My father even posted on Facebook about passing the cradle to me and my kids—the next generation. A book about Sam Maloof's work mentioned how I owned the cradle. My father told other family members with pride that he had passed on the heirloom to me and my kids.

And most painfully, his handwritten notes, found at the desk where he had been shot, stated plainly the cradle was mine.

So you can imagine my agony when his emotions weren't honored. "Dad never updated his will from ages ago, and was murdered while re-doing it, but that's tough on you!" was the attitude. I was devastated. I was upset at the approach, to make a few more bucks by selling the cradle, rather than it remaining in the family. In the years that had passed since his death, I had begged my sisters to change their minds. I even offered to buy it for fair market value—something that was legally mine. My offer was rejected. It was insisted that the cradle be auctioned, where I'd have to compete with the public (and where fees for everyone involved and the auction house would be layered on the price).

I remember well the day of the auction. On the way there, I got a call from an attorney colleague of mine, a tough, seasoned litigator. For small talk, he asked what I was doing that day. I told him the story plainly and honestly—how I was attending an auction to buy back a family heirloom so I could put my baby in it. He burst out crying. This tough litigator, with no ties to the cradle, could not believe the injustice.

After I won the cradle at auction—and I had to overpay dramatically because of a mystery bidder on the telephone who kept driving up the price—Nicole's lawyers ginned up another dispute, this time over how the proceeds would be divided, and who would cover moving expenses and other things like this.

At this point, the disputes over the cradle had taken so long that my daughter Evie, just 1 when my dad was shot, was now riding a bike. My son Joseph had been born and was now a toddler, almost too big to really use it. The delay had deprived us of forming new memories in the family heirloom—something which was my father's express wish.

Finally, defeated, I gave up. It was my mother who convinced me to. She had stopped speaking with my sisters over their behavior. I think it horrified her to see the avarice unfolding after the death of a parent. "Michael," she said. "This cradle means a lot to you, I know. But it's not a piece you can hide. It's not like a watch or even a painting, which you can look at when you want. You will have to walk past it in your living room every day. And when you do, it will be hard to remember the good times with your father, and hard to escape the pain of his murder and the subsequent ordeal over this heirloom."

I finally told everyone that I was done. The cradle sold again at a second auction for much less, and everyone pocketed a few thousand bucks.

As part of the legal filings in 2019, I held little back. Despite being in public office, I was a private person, and hadn't share many of the details. But I refuted to the court the notion that *I* had drawn any suspicions on anyone, or that *I* had been the source of perceptions of greed. And I submitted under penalty of perjury many of the colorful details of my father's last days that the detectives had been miffed at me for not sharing fully.

A NEW TEAM

Shortly thereafter, I received an e-mail from the LAPD. The previous detectives had been pulled off the case. Two new detectives were assigned to it. Would I be so kind as to meet with them sometime?

I met with them the next week. They had read my court filing, and were now very conciliatory. Gone was any notion that I was holding anything back. Absent from the new team was the chauvinism and aggressiveness, and the odd attacks on the media.

The new detectives were fantastic. One of them, veteran detective Grace Thornton, was one of the most compassionate people I've ever met in law enforcement. She was great, and I could tell that she genuinely cared about victims and their families.

Her partner, Luis Romero, was absolutely first rate. I sensed in him the quiet patience and attention to detail that make a good detective. He was clearly proud of his craft, and dedicated to doing a good job. He told me in one subsequent encounter that solving my father's case would make him feel complete if he retired.

I was happy. In the course of our meeting, we discussed everything, in an open and free-wheeling manner. They seemed to be putting new eyes on things, and approaching things from a fresh perspective.

Through all the years, I had often been asked why I hadn't gotten more political. Why I hadn't complained or grandstanded in the media. Given the crappy service, the bad bedside manner of the previous detectives, their lack of cooperation with and hostility towards the media, and the awful things they put me through—why had I not pulled a power play and gone to my friends in the city, insisting that heads should roll? The simple answer is: That's not now I carry myself. Yes, I was close to the Mayor, and had served in the Legislature with half of the city council. I have contacts high up throughout the Los Angeles police department, and in other departments around the region. But my integrity means everything to me. I refuse to be "that guy"—asking for special treatment, or breeding resentment by pulling rank all the time. And I don't want to be seen to politicize my father's death by involving politicians in the process. After much time, the system had done what I would have asked for anyway. I just had to bear some pain on the road. It opened my eyes to what victims' families deal with all the time.

After much time, the system had worked. It had done what I would have asked for anyway. I just had to bear some pain along the road. It opened my eyes to what victims' families deal with, all the time.

The new detectives wanted to speak with a few of my father's friends and relatives. Mind you, this was something me and my friends had begged the previous detectives to do. They asked me for contact phone numbers of my father's key friends and relatives, with whom he had discussed matters like how he spent his days, his associates, his estate plans, etc. right before his death. On this topic, I felt a little angry and regretful about the lost opportunities. My father was almost eighty when he was murdered. Just given his peer group, and with the passage of time, his close friends and relatives were all in their eighties or nineties, and one was over one hundred. Memories fade, especially at that age. This to me was frustrating.

I also connected the detectives with a legendary genetic genealogist who I had asked for advice over the years. She had solved over one-hundred cases, and had offered to help here. One of her best traits was taking complex concept and expressing them in a way that everyone could understand. She certainly helped me.

The new detectives being on the case inaugurated a renaissance of sorts. Late 2019 and early 2020 were marked by a flourish of activity on this now cold case. I connected them with another outside genealogist and investigator who could help them work through difficult DNA issues. I raised again the idea (which had been confirmed by giant DNA lab Thermo Fisher) that one could infer a criminal's surname based on publicly available Y-STR profiles. I was contacted by several media outlets, from Project Cold Case, to NBC's Dateline, about helping to highlight my dad's case. I remember thinking in early 2020 that we were making real progress.

INVESTIGATING A CASE
DURING A PANDEMIC

COVID-19 threw a wrench in everything, including of course the investigation. Like with everything else, things kept going, but at limited productivity. Teams couldn't meet in person and brainstorm. Personnel got called off on other matters. People working from home did not have access to the same things they did at their workplaces. Plus everyone was just....distracted by it all.

I tried mightily to maintain the momentum, but it was hard. The only major news was bad. I had been working with the fantastic Deputy District Attorney assigned to my father's case to try to expand the DNA testing they could do, notably to search genealogy websites. Working with the police, they had contacted the most cutting-edge labs, but they had confirmed—the sample was just too small and too fragmented to be of much use. This was heartbreaking. We had all hoped this would lead to the breakthrough that would have solved the case.

ANOTHER MISSED MILESTONE

In 2021, at a dazzling ceremony in Geneva, Switzerland (which was moved from Rome due to the pandemic), I was knighted by the Royal House of Savoy, Italy's former ruling family. Specifically, I was formally inducted into the Order of Saints Maurice & Lazarus, the second-oldest order of knighthood in the world, and one of the rare orders of knighthood recognized by papal bull. The royal house knighted me for my work promoting Italian culture, my service to the people of California in the Legislature, my work with the house of Savoy, and my philanthropic efforts.

The order of St. Lazarus was created in AD 1098 to protect sick pilgrims in Jerusalem. The younger half, the order of St. Maurice, dates to 1434. Pope Gregory the XIII issued two important papal bulls during his tenure: One reconfirmed the vitality of both orders and gave the House of Savoy the right to confer both knighthoods in perpetuity. The other papal bull put in place the modern calendar.

The orders were merged shortly thereafter, with a mandate to defend Italian shores and to continue to assist the sick. The knights fought some interesting battles throughout history, including one "on the shores of Tripoli", alongside the United States Marines, which of course, adopted that phrasing for their hymn.

It was a profound honor, right up there with getting elected to serve the people of California. My father would've been so proud. We had some noble blood way back in our heritage, descending from a noted Southern Italian *condottiere*. But for the last several centuries, my people had been simple farmers and laborers. And now I was a member of this ancient order. As I thought about how much my father would have liked to see this day, I vowed to continue to strive to make him proud, even if he wasn't here to experience such things in person.

EPIPHANIES...
AND MORE CONFUSION

In May 2022, the world had re-opened after Covid. It was time to do another in-person meeting with the police. I asked for and received another meeting with Luis Romero, the dedicated, intuitive, and thorough detective who was one of the two main investigators on the case.

I'm not sure why, but it was only in this conversation with him that things gelled. I had learned some of these things before, in bits and pieces. But only after this conversation, and with the benefit of so much time and reflection, did things become a little clearer. But unfortunately, the epiphanies just led to more questions.

At the beginning of our meeting, I learned something new. Something very significant. I don't remember if I had asked this before, and it certainly had not been volunteered. There was gunshot residue on my father's hands and arms. Gunshot residue can consist of both burned and unburned gunpowder traces. This tends to indicate that either the gun was my father's, and the murderer had wrestled it away from him. Or that my father fought back.

PROCESSING THE
NEW INFORMATION

After I put aside my shock that I was only learning this nine years after the murder, I tried to consider the ramifications of each possibility in turn. The previous detectives had asked me if my father owned a gun, and they had found a few old ones at his house. The new detective further told me that the ammunition in the gun was "old" (meaning dated). To me, this inference explained why I remember one journalist, likely with LAPD sources, being so keen on determining if my father owned a gun, going so far as to look at my parent's divorce records to determine so.

But it was still highly problematic. My father was a huge proponent of gun safety and loved my young nephew, then 19-years-old, who came over often. It is unlikely he kept a gun in the open, or even nearby. If the gun was my father's, and the killer was the car burglar, this would also create a new problem: that of two guns.

Folks holding handguns properly can't engage in a wrestling match.

Finally, my father was a beast. He had the hand strength of guys half his age. You have to understand that I'm a very muscular, very strong person myself, and I am merely a slender, diluted version of my dad when it comes to hand strength. He had giant wrists and giant hands. I don't think he could have had a gun wrested from him, especially to such a degree that one pointed at an intruder was next pointing at himself.

Next the new detective and I discussed at length the things that had always bothered me. Recall some of the questions I posed previously: How many petty thieves enter an obviously occupied house with three cars outside and lights on? How many rush into the one room where someone obviously is? How many people stick around after a very loud gunshot in close quarters? (A neighbor could have called 911 for all you know). How many people have the awful gumption to sit there while a man bleeds to death, and try to break into safes and the like, sitting there with a corpse? (We've all seen the movies where a gunshot victim passes out, only to awake suddenly and fight back or call 911).

The detective said to me a few words that at least partially vindicated the logic I had agonized over for years. "You're probably right." He said that he did not believe the timeline. He said it was way more likely that my father had surprised the burglar, who had done all the ransacking *before* he shot my dad. That the burglar had likely fled the minute the gun went off. That explains why there was only one shot, and why so little, including things that were obviously valuable were taken. The killer had likely not stuck around. Not being a doctor, he had no way of knowing the bullet had severed an artery. This scenario (my father surprised the burglar), we agreed, was way more consistent with human behavior.

But frustratingly, it just led to more questions and more inconsistencies. Recall that my father's bedroom had one way in, one way out. After coming home, he would have walked upstairs in a very open and airy entryway, and entered his bedroom. Recall too, that there were signs of obvious ransacking: a file cabinet hacked open, and jewelry envelopes strewn everywhere, among other things.

My father was no dummy. If he came home and saw a room obviously ransacked, he'd be likely to turn around, walk outside (which would have taken maybe 10 seconds), and dial 911. He would not try to unlock a safe to get to a gun. It is doubtful he would stick around.

Unless he recognized the intruder.

Now, I suppose a burglar could have hidden when he heard my father returning, and then jumped out with a gun pointed to his head. But now we're getting to inferences upon inferences. Besides, from what I knew from the detectives about the trajectory of the bullet, my father was likely shot while already sitting down. It was all quite confusing.

We know my father came home, tried to set up the printer, and likely tooled around on his computer between say 6:30 and 7:30pm. We know the ransacking would take at least an hour. So we would still need to explain where my father went during that time. He wasn't the type to have a weekday restaurant dinner with a friend—and if so, that person would have come forward. I believe the cops ruled out him getting gas (and why not get that when on the way home, for that matter?) My father did pay cash for things, but he kept receipts. That's how they knew he had been to Costco. There were no other receipts of which I'm aware.

We also can rule out my father taking a walk. With so much media coverage, especially in the community, any of the hundreds of people who would have seen him walking that night would have stepped forward. If I had to guess, I could conceive of my father working to set up the printer, and then dashing out to Staples because he needed another cord or some more toner or paper, where, perhaps, he ended up not buying anything after all.

Is it possible the killer had an accomplice? That some kind of hybrid theory is the truth? That someone my dad knew knocked on his door, and said, "let's go get coffee" while someone else tried to knock off his house? But then my father returned early, and the person accidentally shot him? I suppose anything could be true.

Either way, we still need to explain how my dad ended up in the deepest corner of the room, sitting at his desk, where the likely shot occurred. Yes, the killer could have made him sit, or he could have tried to make it to his land line, but neither make much sense. If the burglar surprised him, it was more likely to be by the door—and that is where my father should have been found—especially if there was a wrestling match, explaining the residue.

In sum, there is a problem with every theory. The necessary inferences one must draw from various facts make it impossible to synthesize them all.

MORE NEW THEORIES?

At time of writing, my father's case is a cold case that has stretched over a decade. As you can tell by the contents of this book, I've obsessed about it for much of that time. I like to think I've considered every theory, including the most painful and the most wacky. That's why I was so shocked when in a conversation in January 2023, I heard a new one—or really two new ones—for the first time. As always, the conversation with the new detective on the case was helpful, and interesting.

After I expressed to him all the above—that I had had time to process all the information, and that I still saw defects in most of the theories, he shared a new profile, with two intriguing possibilities, which none of us had really seriously considered all this time. First, that the killer could have indeed been a business associate of my dad's—likely some old guy who was not all there or had some kind of business dispute with my dad. This profile, which the detective raised, was an older guy who maybe met my dad at a jewelry show and was desperate for cash, or an older guy, perhaps even a friend, who had had a falling out with my dad. Second, the detective stated that my father may have been placed on his chair by the perpetrator, like "there now"—which the detective said is actually common when the perpetrator knows the suspect. (Apparently some murderers who know their victim even lay them on a bed or pull a sheet over them!)

This "normal old guy that my dad knew" theory would explain a lot…. Why the perpetrator had no record. Why the perpetrator had not re-offended—he could be a non-criminal, or he could be dead. Why the gun and the ammunition were "old"—an "old man's weapon." Why my dad maybe tried to wrestle away the weapon.

However, no theory is perfect, and this one still had defects. Yes, if this was someone my father knew from his jewelry business, or a friend, my father would have opened the door, and that would explain why there was no forced entry. However, it would not explain my father letting him up into the third floor—which remember, he didn't even let his housekeeper clean. And we'd be right back to the very problematic fact, which has always bothered me: if my dad let this person in, that means that the hour's worth of ransacking would need to have occurred after my dad was shot— meaning we'd be right back to the ridiculous notion that a non-criminal fired a gun in an enclosed space, and then sat there while my father died. That to me is still problematic (1) due to the capacity for people to panic after a gunshot, particularly an accidental one; (2) because people tend to believe everyone heard what they did, and the perpetrator would have no idea that police weren't called after a noisy "bang!"; and (3) the odd trait of working in a room while someone bleeds to death. No, if my dad opened the door for a friend, you still have those problems.

You also still have the problems of the perpetrator trying to open a safe with garden shears or a fireplace poker. Again, these were strong safes, those very thick, very heavy safes you see in the movies. You'd have to be really high, really stupid, or really staging the crime scene, to try to get into those safes with such tools. And generally speaking, I see such an act, if genuine, as the misguided attempt by a dumb kid—not some old guy who has seen the old westerns where even gunshots fail to open such safes.

So, while these new theories were helpful in that they imparted additional humility into my thinking—I haven't yet thought of *everything*—they continue to be sources of logical and emotional frustration.

THE PLIGHT OF OTHER VICTIMS

In late 2021, I attended a memorable march to bring awareness to crime victims. We met on the streets of South Los Angeles, and walked several miles with our signs and posters of our family members that had been murdered. I had attended dozens of these marches and rallies since my father's murder, but this one stood out because of a woman I met.

Speaking at this rally was a mother whose son had recently been shot by gang members because they thought one of their girlfriends liked him. He died in her arms on their front lawn. "Mama…It hurts," had been his last words. This mother spoke about how everyone in her community seemed to know exactly who had killed her son, and yet how the police had yet to seriously press the issue. There was something about her tears that spoke to me. Recognizing the rawness in her emotions, I tried as best as I could to comfort her, while also knowing that what she was going through was harder than my experiences.

There was only so much I could do. "Does it get easier?" she asked me. "Yes," I replied. "The passage of time dulls your grief a little." But for her next series of questions that day, I had nothing great for her. "Do you ever miss your dad less," she asked? "No," I replied, honestly. "The passage of time doesn't make you miss your departed loved one any less, nor does it impart in you any profound sense of meaning." The fact that my father's killer had yet to be brought to justice also forced me to answer her questions honestly about that topic too. But I told her to keep the faith, and that I hoped her son's killers would be brought to justice.

We exchanged phone numbers and kept in contact. Many times, she'd call me crying, and I'd just do my best to listen, express empathy, and try to help her work through the difficult emotions she felt at the moment. I know what she was going through was infinitely harder than my experiences, and I felt like I owed it to her to help her, when she felt like society had turned its back.

Yet a few months later, I got a message from her at 3:30 in the morning one night. Her message read, "I'm sorry to bother you at this time But honestly I need someone, I don't think I can keep going I feel so alone without my son. I'm sorry I don't know who to call of where to go.. I'm alone in [the] streets and I just don't know what to do." I called her as soon as I got the message. It went to voice mail. I texted her. My texts went unanswered.

THE CONTINUING STATE OF THINGS

The murder rate in Los Angeles has risen markedly since 2013. All violent crimes are up, in fact. And this is in a city where the population is often so jaded, people don't report crimes any more. My father lived through Los Angeles' classic noir era, and I lived through its "typical big city" era. But he was killed in its golden era of low crime. I am sad that a fourth era, of again rising crime, appears to be upon us.

48% of murders in California go unsolved. In Los Angeles, that number has risen to be slightly over 50%. It's amazing to me that it's basically a coin flip that those commit murder—the most heinous of crimes—will never be brought to justice. Note that in Sweden, 80% of murders are solved, and in Finland, Japan, and South Korea, upwards of 95% are.

It's also amazing to me how the murder-clearance rate has gone down in the era of DNA. And I wonder if ironically, that's because of DNA. All around the country, police forces can often just wait for a DNA match, instead of engaging in the gumshoe tactics of old: speaking with people, and letting one brainstorm and one clue lead to another, and then another.

As I was writing this book, I got contacted by a former art model who had worked in my father's classrooms. She was so nice, and it was clear to me that she missed him so much. She wrote a beautiful poem about my father's case, and it was deeply touching.

She encouraged me to ask my dad to come to me in my dreams, and offered to try to solve his case using astrology. I've tried the former with little luck, and I suppose I'd entertain the latter.

Also as I was writing this book, the occasional insensitive, crazy calls continued. One summer day I received a call from a lady who knew many of the same people I knew; enough to sound credible at first. She proceeded to tell me that my father was killed by a crime ring that was run by an elderly, retired politician (and dear friend of mine), working with an elderly, retired plaintiff's attorney. Then, of course, she asked me for help re-opening her divorce proceedings against one of them. I don't think these folks care about the pain they cause. But I wish they knew how crazy they sounded.

NON DENOUEMENT

In August 2023, my father's estate finally settled, and I received the final disbursement check, for about $1000. I shudder to think how my father would view the attorneys and others who made a simple teacher's estate so complicated.

November 2023 marked the tenth anniversary of my father's death. I still have more questions than answers.

To this day, Novembers are hard. Every year, leading up to the 12th, I find myself plagued by inescapable sadness. It sounds silly since it's been so long. I can't explain it, other than the time of year forces my subconscious to think about my father dying alone, bleeding out from a gunshot wound — and the fact that we still haven't brought anyone to justice.

And since his death, right up until the present time, if I haven't seen someone for a while, the conversation goes something like this:

"Great to see you, Mike! It's been a while."

"How have you been? What are you up to? How are your kids?"

Then, inevitably, there is a pregnant pause.

"Say...did they ever catch whoever did that to your dad?"

And then the expressions of disbelief follow.

With so few concrete answers, it's possible to come up with any scenario that fits your predilections. The boy could have correctly seen a gun in the hands of the car burglar. The car burglar could have owned an older weapon with older ammo. My dad could have left his house after coming home, purchased nothing, and returned to surprise the car burglar, resulting in a wrestling match and an accidental discharge. But as I noted herein, each scenario has its problems. None is perfect.

For me it's very hard to believe that a criminal who was so dumb as to leave so much physical evidence on so many different items has not re-offended. "He could be dead," people say. Yes. And that would prevent us from ever seeing any justice, or knowing what really happened on that crisp November night.

As of writing, new DNA advances are happening all the time. Law enforcement can try to match samples with those of relatives uploaded to publicly available familial-matching sites. But with small or fragmented samples, the process is long and frustrating.

I miss my father, and although I'm neither overly religious or superstitious, I sometimes pray to him in heaven:

"Please help me be a good father with no regrets. Please protect your family here on earth. And please let us someday learn who ripped you from our family."

ABOUT THE AUTHOR

Mike Gatto represented Hollywood and surrounding areas for seven years in the California Legislature. Before being elected, he served as a Congressional Chief of Staff, and in the administrations of three Los Angeles Mayors. He's the Managing Partner of Actium LLP, a law firm, and is a fixture in the media, as a commentator on national news talk shows. He lives in the Los Angeles area with his wife and three children.

NOTE FROM MIKE GATTO

Word-of-mouth is crucial for any author to succeed. If you enjoyed *Noir by Necessity*, please leave a review online—anywhere you are able. Even if it's just a sentence or two. It would make all the difference and would be very much appreciated.

Thanks!
Mike Gatto

We hope you enjoyed reading this title from:

BLACK ROSE
writing™

www.blackrosewriting.com

Subscribe to our mailing list – *The Rosevine* – and receive
FREE books, daily deals, and stay current with news about
upcoming releases and our hottest authors.
Scan the QR code below to sign up.

Already a subscriber? Please accept a sincere thank you for
being a fan of Black Rose Writing authors.

View other Black Rose Writing titles at
www.blackrosewriting.com/books and use promo
code
PRINT to receive a **20% discount** when purchasing.

9 781685 133318